ROTTEN HAYSTACKS

More than 870 *new* limericks

JOHN SLIM

Illustrated by
COLIN WHITTOCK

Foreword by
GYLES BRANDRETH

Published by Underwood Enterprises

British Library Cataloguing in Publication Data
A catalogue record for this book is available
from the British Library

Also by John Slim, published by Underwood Enterprises:
Rather Rottener -
More than 900 *naughty* new limericks

Printed and designed by Cerebus Communications
Published by Underwood Enterprises
47 Alcester Road, Lickey End, Bromsgrove B60 1JT
Telephone & Fax 01527 559221.
ISBN 0-9537613-0-4

CONTENTS

CONTENTS - 2

***

FOREWORD

By Gyles Brandreth

THERE was a young lady named Zanka
Who retired while the ship lay at anchor,
    But awoke in dismay
    When she heard the mate say,
"We must pull up the top sheet and spanker."

A limerick, as you probably know, is a five-line nonsense verse that originated with the 18th-century alehouse chorus, *Will you come up to Limerick.* As a form of poetry, it was made famous by Edward Lear.

Although at the limericks of Lear
We may sometimes be tempted to sneer,
    We should never forget
    That we owe him a debt
For his work as the first pioneer.

The trouble with Lear's limericks is that they tend to be remarkably respectable:

There was an old person from Twickenham
Who whipped his four horses to quicken 'em.
    When they stood on one leg,
    He said faintly, "I beg
We may go back directly to Twickenham."

And the trouble with respectable limericks is that they tend to be somewhat short on laughs:

The limerick packs laughs anatomical
Into space that is quite economical,
    But the good ones I've seen
    So seldom are clean
And the clean ones so seldom are comical.

Why? Well. . .

The limerick form is complex.
Its contents run chiefly to sex.
    It burgeons with virgeons
    And masculine urgeons
And swarms with erotic effects.

As you can tell, I recognise a quality limerick when I see one, but in truth I hadn't seen that many until I came across the works of John Slim.

Mr Slim is an extraordinary phenomenon: a distinguished journalist, a writer of elegant prose; but most of all, best of all, the Laureate of the Limerick!

He must deserve a place in *The Guinness Book of Records as the author of more original limericks than any other writer on the planet. He deserves a place in *The Oxford Book of Verse* as a unique poet with a remarkable capacity for encapsulating all human life in a mere five lines.**

Dear reader, in your hands you have one volume of the *War and Peace* of pint-sized poetry. With its companion volume, *Rotten Haystacks*, it represents an extraordinary four years' work of the Tolstoy of rhyme. It is, quite simply, a Slim volume like no other. Enjoy!

Gyles Brandreth.

* Alas for this happy thought, having been confronted by 1,700 brand new limericks, the Guinness Editorial Department said that "this was not a category which the editorial committee decided to monitor." - J S.

AUTHOR'S NOTE

IT is a little disconcerting when truths that have been handed down from generation to generation start to crumble. That's how it was for me with The Orange Cushion Month Myth.

When I was assured, as a not-particularly-interested mixed infant, that *orange, cushion* and *month* were the only words in the English language with which no other words rhymed, I did not question it. I went on not questioning it and then I didn't question it some more.

The truth did not dawn until I was well into the task of tackling *Rotten Haystacks* and *Rather Rottener*. You cannot endure the frustrations inherent in composing some 1,800 limericks without starting to suspect that The Orange Cushion Month Myth has got it wrong.

While I had no idea how many words *really* would not rhyme with any other words, I was confident that there were more than three - even though *orange*, courtesy of *lozenge*, turned out to be a non-starter after all. Eventually, I sat up in bed for 20 minutes to think, and wrote down 50.

Else, flange, lemon, fondle, golf, rugby, kingdom, argue, subtlety, clothes, eastern, western, northern, southern, sixty, seventy, ninety, thousand, partner, filthy . . .

And the rest.

There are dozens of them. It does not matter that you are concerned only with failures to make good, honest rhymes and will not let assonance into the equation with its interesting insistence that *comedy*, for instance, could not be considered a non-rhymer because it rhymes with *swaddling* and that *admiral* is a ready-made partner for *halogen*.

It was immediately obvious that uncovering non-rhymers offered no challenge - there's another one - so the next stage was to find unrhymable pairs:

English breakfast. Roman orgy. Chocolate soldier. Personal snapshot. Bishop's homily. Lunatic asylum. Social circle. . . and so on. Much more fun!

From there, emerged unrhymable headlines:

Hungry dolphins menace women. Chaos threatens hospital. . .

Time, I think, with long winter evenings in mind, to start work on the unrhymable novel. But not, perhaps, just yet.

John Slim

INTRODUCTION

Limericks have never quite been
Regarded as spotlessly clean:
Their aim is to stay,
In their own wicked way,
Naughty and sporty and mean.

But Homer, they say, sometimes nods -
Which is why now, despite all the odds,
As clean as a whistle
And fit for a missal,
Is verse to please ancients and mods.

Among that which follows, you can
Find several examples which scan
And rhyme, when rehearsed,
Right way round AND reversed -
Which is new in the limerick span.

Another departure you'll see
Is the limerick-anagram: be
Prepared for a game
With the odd jumbled name.
A verse may contain up to three.

Moreover, without cock and bull,
Or effort at pulling the wool,
It's meet to point out
Three verses about
Llanfair PG - spelled in full!

Tongue-twisters to tie you in knots,
Scathing remarks about clots
Whose lunacies send

INTRODUCTION - 2

Us all round the bend -
They've all been allotted their slots.

There's plenty of word play as well,
And verses which rhyme as they spell
Words letter by letter
And finally get a
Gradual sentence to gel.

If you grieve that they're clean, please take heart,
For this book is only the start.
There's a whole load of terse
And original verse
Which is loyal to the limerick art.

This volume is simply like snow -
Pure as the driven - although.
If you DO want a blush
And a wade through some slush,
A second book's out on the go.

In verses, together they make
Eighteen hundred or more and they take
The limerick form
Away from the norm,
With chuckles as well (by mistake).

***

THE PEOPLE AND PLACES

Appearing in verse in these pages are:

THE PEOPLE

FRED; plus
Abel, Adam, Woody Allen, Amanda, Americans, Anne, Anstruther, Antony, Archimedes, Auntie, Bach, Beethoven, Bill, Monocle Bill the Sailor, Bizet, Tony Blair, Anne Boleyn, Botticelli, Brahms, the Rev Chris Brain, Brenda, the Brit, Britons, Brummel, Burlington-Burke, Rabbie Burns, J Caesar, Cain, Canute, Truman Capote, the Chair, Chantelle, Charles, Charley, Chas, Chaucer, Chinaman, Chinese, Chopin, Cindy, Clare, Santa Claus, Cleopatra, Clive, John Constable, Consumer (Confused), Cordelia, Fanny Cradock, Creation, Dad, Dan, Dante, David, Dawn, Lord Derby, The Devil, Dewar, Di, Diane, Dick, the Doctor, Dorothy, a Drwyd, the Duke, Edmund, T S Eliot, Elvis, Eva, Eve, Fanny, Father, Fawkes, Fifi, a Finn, Frame, Frank, Uncle Fred, Gary, Paul Gascoigne, Gawd, Gazza, Germans, Geste, Farmer Giles, Gloucester, Old Gobbo, God, Goliath, Goneril, Gooch, The Great Charmer, Hugh Green, Gus, Hal, Harold, Harry, Hector, A Herman, Henry VIII, Henry the Pooch, James Hewitt, Henry Higgins, His Honour, Hogg, Sherlock Holmes, Homer, Mother Hubbard, Humpty, Island Frank, Ivanhoe, Jack, Great Aunt Jane, Dr Jekyll, Joan of Arc, Job, Joe, Tokyo Joe, Jonah, Jones, Josiah, Kate, Katie, Keith, Nancy Kerrigan, King Harold, King's Men, Kipling, Labour, Lear, Edward Lear, King Lear, The Left, Alan Jay Lerner, Liz, Loewe, The Lord, Lot, Lottie, Louise, the MO, MPs, the Rev Paddy McGill, McLeod, Macbeth, Maisie, Mandy, Mark, a Martian, Mather, Matt, David Mellor, the Merchant of Venice, Michael, Michelangelo, the Mob, the Monarch, Monet, Moses, Mother, Mickey Mouse, Moss,

Moss Bros, Mozart, Little Miss Muffet. Mum, Naomi, Nature, Newton, Noah, O'Dowd, Oswald, O'Toole, Pa, Pardn'r, Pat, Patricia, Paul, Pausea, the Peg, Beau Pepys, Pete, Saint Peter, Phoebe, Pisans, the Players, Plunkett, a Pole, the Pope, Porter, Prince Andy, the Prince of Wales, Princess Diana, Quasimodo, the Queen, the Rabumps, Tiara Rabump, Ray, Oliver Reed, Regan, Rev Mother, Roget, the Romans, Rory, Rosaline, Rose, Roz, Bertrand Russell, Sally, Sam, Lord Sandwich, Santa, a Sassenach, Saul, a Scot, Sir Walter Scott, General Sedgewick, Sergeant, Shakespeare, Asterix Short, Shylock, Bill Sikes, Simon, the Smiths, Delia Smith, Son, South Africans, Spencer, Stan, Stanley, Steve, Strauss, Sue, Susan, Susie, Sydney, Bill Sykes, Tarzan, Graham Taylor, Ted, William Tell, Terry, Tex, Margaret Thatcher, Thomas Richard, Tolstoy, Tom, Tommy, Toya, Tranter, Tweedle, Vera, George Washington, Wayne, Whatsername, Watson, William, Win, the Wizard of Oz, Wongs, Zoe.

THE PLACES

Abergavenny, Aix-les-Bains, Alaska, Albuquerque, Aldwych, America, Ascot, Bangor, Basildon, Belize, Bicester, Birmingham, Boston, Bourne, Bradley, Braemar, Bray, Bricklehampton, Brighton and Hob, Britain, Brum, Brussels, Buck House, Buckingham Palace, Burnham-on-Sea, Canaan, Chard, Cheam, Cheddar, China, Claridge's, Clee, The Clipper and Cutter, Clovelly, Clun, Clwyd, Cologne, Cork, The Costa, Crewe, Cymbran, Damascus, The Dingle, Disney World, Dolgellau, Dorset, Dover, Dunbar, Dunoon, The Eagle and Star, Ealing, Earth, East Fife, East Sheen, Elba, Emmanuel, England, Essex, Fakenham, Fife, Fleet, Glengarry, Gower, Greenland, Hades, Halifax, Hamilton, Hastings, Hayes, Hell, Herne, Hollywood, Hook, Houston, The Hyatt, Ipswich, Isle of Capri, Istanbul, Italy, Jarrow, Kent, Kenya, Kew, Kings Lynn, Kinsale, Knightsbridge, Lahore, Lea Bank, Leamington Spa, Leek, Leith, Lille, Lincolnshire, Liverpool, Llanfair PG, Llanfairpwllgwysyllgogerychwyrndrobwlltysiliogogogoch, Loch Ness, Looe, Louth, Lake Lugano, Las Vegas, Lydney, Madeira, Madras, Marseille, Mass, Mayfair, Mdx, Nantes, Naples, Nastend, Newnham, New Zealand, Norwich, Oz, Paris, Parkhurst, Parma, Pisa,

The Pond, Porthcawl, Pwllheli, Reading, Redhill, Rheims, Rome, Rouen, Ryde, Rye, St Just, Salisbury Plain, Saskatchewan, Seville, Sheffield, Shoreditch, Siam, Southend, Sutton, The Tate, Tokyo, Torbay, Torquay, Tralee, Troon, Troy, Tucson, Uganda, Valletta, Versaille, Wales, Ware, Wembley, West Looe, Windermere, Wogga Wogga, Zurich.

A HEALTH WARNING

These verses - it's just a suggestion -
Are best in small doses, no question.
    Repetitive rhythm,
    Which they carry whythm,
Could lead to some slight indigestion

Amusing though limericks may be,
At a sitting, don't read more than three.
    As the beat's repetitious,
    In spite of your witious,
You'll find that you'll drop off to slee. . .

***

KING LEAR

Edward Lear knew his verse form was fine.
But he said, "There's a fault in design.
The rhyme scheme's OK -
A-A-B-B-A -
But I shouldn't repeat the first line.

"I fear that it *could* be a bore
Which people will start to deplore.
Rhymes should stay alive
To the end of line five,
But I've put the joke in line four."

All the same, what he did was sincere,
Which is why today's limericks are here.
Were Shakespeare on hand,
He'd quite understand
Why the world likes a laugh with King Lear.

J D S

***

THERE WAS AN OLD KING CALLED LEAR...
Colin W.

ROTTEN HAYSTACKS

Rotten Haystacks: **the title may send**
You intrigued or incensed round the bend.
It's simply some antics
With frantic semantics -
Explained, if you skip to the end.*

* See ***Failed-Again Footnote*** - page 203

FRED

These rhymes need a hero, we thought;
Someone whom life would sell short;
A crass but quite bonhomous,
Never anonymous,
Highly adaptable sort.

These rhymes need a hero, we said -
A thought which remorselessly led,
Except for expansion
Of rhyme schemes or scansion,
To pinning the action on Fred.

***

I

SPORTING GESTURES

A young golfing novice called Clive
Tried to keep all his matches alive:
From the tee he would roll
That small ball to the hole,
Shouting "Fore!", taking ten, writing five.

The paddock at Ascot has gloss:
Top hats and tails - no dross.
All borrowed, perceive -
So who can believe
Strolling roans gather no Moss?

A golfer with fine self-delusion
Never took a spare ball - found confusion.
Straight off the first tee,
Sliced into the sea.
His game was called *Fore!*-gone-conclusion.

An amateur sailor called Porter
Bought a dinghy to sail with his daughter.
They're now seen afloat
With their feet in the boat
And both their backsides in the water.

A golfer's wife got her divorce,
But the man shows no sign of remorse.
He's vulgar, he's lewd,
He's incredibly crude:
His son calls him Pa for the coarse.

Sporting Gestures

Our cricketers don't have to try:
We've a ground that makes visitors cry.
    When it's our turn to bowl,
    Fred jumps in a hole
To catch daisy-cutters waist-high.

    Two racehorses; Salisbury Plain:
    One says, "I am feeling inane!
        It couldn't be sillier!
        You pace is familiar,
    But I just can't remember your mane."

A magnificent batting display
Moved a Russian spectator to say,
    "This ground is too small.
    He keeps hitting the ball
Out of sight - what a waste of a day!"

    Rugby's ball is an oval one, which
    Means its bounce is a bit of a bitch.
        But it's all in the game -
        There's tremendous acclaim
    Whenever it's kicked off the pitch.

Though cricket may have little charm, as
Far as I know, there's no harm, as
    Its aim is not deep:
    It's to send us to sleep.
They play it at night in pyjamas.

    A cricket match can't be all bad.
    There's something in there to be had
        For the expert who dotes -
        And the men in white coats
    Look after the ones it drives mad.

Sporting Gestures

Golfers and anglers all vie
For success in the sport that they try:
Putting and fishing
Are all hope and wishing,
And greatly depend on the lie.

Professional boxers? Insane!
All blood and an addling brain!
An amateur, though,
Is more mad than a pro -
Getting thumped for no monetary gain.

Canals provide sport for the gods:
Fishermen fighting the odds.
A chorus of whines:
Boats caught in their lines,
While walkers fall over their rods.

A boomerang thrower cried, "Hey!
I've played with this object all day!"
He said, with black eyes,
Broken teeth and bruised thighs,
He'd been trying to throw it away.

A saddened old golfer of note
Resigned from his club when he wrote:
"Since I swallowed a ball,
If I hit one at all,
I just get a lump in my throat."

In snooker, when aiming, they call,
"Blue ball!" or *"Brown ball!"* - and yet all
We need is a fellow
To call out, say, *"Yellow!"*
We've already guessed it's a ball.

Sporting Gestures

Geriatric must be what one calls
A feat that's inscribed in fame's halls
When Germans play cricket
And one takes a wicket
Three times in consecutive balls.

Croquet is cruel, not polite.
It's a joust, not genteel: it's a fight!
How low people stoop!
You're in line for your hoop -
And your ball's simply slammed out of sight.

A tenor sax scrum-half sought fun
With a mixed-doubles alto from Clun.
His swinging, her serving,
Her singing, his swerving,
Made both wish they'd never begun.

"Put your shirt on that horse", they all said.
"Be alert! A dead cert! Go ahead!"
That horse, but of course,
Was a source of remorse:
Dead cert much less certain than dead.

Said a peg-legged groundsman, "I force
My golfers to show great resource:
More holes on each green
Than ever they've seen,
Plus ten thousand out on the course."

Simon will climb and then stop.
Simon the climber's a flop!
We've seen Simon climb a
Hill timon timba-
gain without reaching the top.

Sporting Gestures

A yachtsman, just back from the seas,
Said, "Everything went like a breeze.
One of the arts
Is to study your charts
And get yourself home by degrees."

Said a racehorse, "It's got out of hand,
How jockeys - a bright little band -
Seem unable to see
There's a saddle on me,
So though they could sit, they all stand."

A balding old cyclist said,
"The slats in my helmet have led
Some folks to begin
To regard with a grin
The sunburn in stripes on my head."

TWO OF A KIND

Swimming's a pleasure: you get
Such excellent exercise - yet
The insuperable snag
Is a bit of a drag:
You always get awfully wet

Though swimming is fun, don't forget
There's a drawback that's not been solved yet.
When one's having a ball
With breast stroke or crawl,
One always gets dreadfully wet.

Sporting Gestures

A referee out on the pitch
Seemed to have an incurable itch.
        Throughout every match,
        He did nothing but scratch,
But he said it was digital twitch.

        It's as well that two men of resource
        Didn't swap over interests, of course.
                Lords Derby and Sandwich
                Gave their names to the language:
        We could have been snacking on horse.

A quiet young man from Cologne
Is the loneliest fellow we've known.
        He bucks all the trends
        By not making friends,
And he synchronize-swims on his own.

***

II

LITERARY LEANINGS

RABBIE BURNS, it is clear, didn't care.
He dashed off his poems with flair.
In one of his best,
Tim'rous beast rhymes with *breast*
And *hastily*, just for a dare.

Rabbie Burns, that implacable poet,
Rhymed *beast* with *breast* and *hastily*.
He brought down the house
With his tim'rous rodent.
Now I'm rhyming *gasworks* with *bicycle*.

THE LIMERICK

***There was a* - the usual way**
Of launching a limerick lay -
Can never ring true,
Alas, because who
Stresses *was* when he speaks day-to-day?

The limerick does not rely
On status in any way high.
Yet somehow its form
Takes people by storm -
And nobody understands why

There's a clock-watching poet in Kew,
Whose limericks end at line two.

Literary Leanings

Macbeth is a thane full of pain,
And he stays in the main on the wane,
With strife with his wife
And a ghost and a knife,
Three witches and half the cast slain.

POETRY LESSON

Poems today, heaven knows,
Are simple to write, and it shows.
You don't need a rhyme
Or scansion or time:
You just have to chop up some prose.

Moreover, there's no-one who'll haggle
If lines have one word or a gaggle.
Ensure there's no form -
Without shape, it's the norm,
And it slops down the page in a straggle.

Likewise, the content's an art.
You don't have to speak from the heart:
Just keep it tendentious
And nice and pretentious,
As if you've some truth to impart.

Poems today rarely rhyme:
Just think of the trouble that saves.
You chop up some prose
And say that it's verse,
And you don't have to struggle with scansion,
either.

Said an idle young man from Tralee,
"My limericks end at line three.
This causes surprise."

Literary Leanings

The Merchant of Venice's nausea
Is eased by a lady named Pausea:
        "Shylock's name will be mud
        If he dare spill your blood.
You don't have to die: he can't fausea."

Dr Jekyll can not be espied:
We knew he'd not be at our side.
        We asked, "Where the hekyll
        We find Dr Jekyll?"
And he told us, "I'm Jekyll and hide."

N-T makes a sound past the ken
Of Hollywood's women and men.
        Transatlannic dismay
        In Shakespeare's play:
The winner of their disconnen?

War and Peace is a novel extending
To hundreds of pages and lending
        To Tolstoy great fame,
        In spite of his claim
That it grew while he searched for an ending.

Don't read it, but actually SEE *Lear*:
There's Goneril, Regan, Cordelia,
        Lear, Gloucester and Ed-
        mund ending up dead,
Like Oswald - but no necrophilia.

A humourless poet, a bore,
Says, "My limericks end at line four.
        It's a form I invoke
        So I don't need a joke."

Literary Leanings

For Bertrand, an annual thing
Was to give people's doorbells a ring
On March Twenty-first,
With a line he'd rehearsed:
"Hello! I'm the Russell of spring."

In *The Merchant of Venice*, we saw
That the Bard had bequeathed us a flaw.
The Venetian blind man,
Old Gobbo, began
To sound like he sold door-to-door.

Quasimodo was not pleased at all
At being involved in a brawl
With footballing lads
Who came with their dads
And said he was hiding the ball.

A limerick writer in Looe
Complained that he hadn't a clue.
"This is my first.
I've never rehearsed.
I can't seem to manage line two."

Some funding would help to endorse a
Spot of research into Chaucer,
To learn why his name
Can rumbustiously claim
Just three words that rhyme, and one's *coarser*.

When there's a strange tale to relate,
Concerning the workings of fate,
Or dire situations
With weird complications,
The limerick gives it you straight.

Literary Leanings

A clever young chap in The Dingle
Claimed fame for his name through the jingle.
He turned out a glut
Of astonishing smut.
Entendres were always just single.

Episcopal purple's not fair:
It simply won't rhyme anywhere.
With its bounce and its zing
And alliterative swing,
It's enough to make poets despair.

Sherlock Holmes always worked out the plots on
All kinds of crimes with old Watson.
He was not known to cease
Knocking spots off police,
And he sorted a band* that had spots on.

* ie, *The Speckled Band.*

Eight beats make this limerick line,
Though at times one will settle for nine.
With five in line three,
Then these six, you can see
Eight more to end up with are fine.

An innumerate lad from Southend
Found his limericks couldn't depend
On his counting to five,
So they all stayed alive
Well after they'd got to the end,
Because they were prone to extend
Until he was stopped by a friend,
Who told him his format should blend
With the commonly recognised trend.

III

ALL FOR ART

MICHELANGELO - he was a sweetie -
Decided to do something meaty.
Inside the Sistine,
Where all was pristine,
Alas, he invented *graffiti.*

An old man, whose scribble-filled start
At a life class could not be called smart,
Said, "Tell you the truth,
I am long in the tooth,
But nobody's younger at art."

The phone rang on stage as the cue
For the words that he hoped that he knew.
He grabbed it, but dried -
And artfully cried
To somebody else, *"It's for you!"**

* This is alleged to have been an incident in the career of A E Matthews, who became notorious for forgetting his lines.

Modern Art caused a hell of a stir.
We just didn't know where we were.
At first, we would say,
"Which way up's the right way?"
Now we hang it the way we prefer.

Botticelli, we're happy to say,
Spurned bronze, alabaster and clay.
If he'd made a statue,
It would turn out so fat you
Could walk round in stages all day.

All for Art

"What a pain my profession has been!"
Cried an artist who lived in East Sheen.
    "Which is true?" asked the fellow.
    "Blue is green mixed with yellow?
Or blue mixed with yellow is green?"

In Parma, an actor named Sam
Is a shallow and blustering sham.
    He's strutting, intoning,
    While everyone's groaning:
He's simply an old Parma ham.

The Players have done it again.
Their audience has to explain
    They're known in the West
    For doing their best
And striving to reach the mundane.

Said an actor in Burnham-on-Sea,
"Though I'm shy and as quiet as can be,
    My thespian art
    May give you a start."
And he laughed with maniacal glee.

The artist asked, "Will you allow
Me to visit, to paint your prize cow?"
    But the farmer demurred:
    "She's the pride of the herd.
I like her the way she is now."

As he painted his ultimate poppy,
Monet said, "Let us make experts stroppy
    With a note saying, 'Right!
    Time to curb your delight!
Start looking, chaps, this one's a copy'."

All for Art

John Constable said, "There might be
A different opinion of me,
If I wrote with my quill
Underneath *Flatford Mill*,
'Painted by numbers - J C'."

As the stars of the show took a bough,
It was clear they were having a rough.
Said one, "That's enough!
Your acting is dough -
And I think you're a silly old cough!"

A dainty young dancer from Clwyd,
Whose movements were graceful and fluid,
Went on to repeat
Her feats on her feet,
Complete with a sheet, as a druid.

The singer is old, but his vocals
Keep being rehearsed for the locals.
His notes are attacked
In a voice that is cracked,
And the gleam in his eye's his bifocals.

There's a wonderful scheme at the Tate:
They'll pile up the bricks while you wait.
They say that it's art
And they come *à la* cart
(So the cart can be Exhibit Eight).

Some painters achieve world renown -
And escape being run out of town -
By splodging a mess
So no-one can guess
If the canvas is hung upside-down.

All for Art

Although Riverdance is upbeat,
It's not very hard to repeat.
    We sat down to shiver
    With shoulders a-quiver -
And next week, we'll sort out the feet.

One thing we discover, alas, is
Regrets do no good as time passes.
    Van Gogh made it clear,
    If you cut off one ear,
There's no way you'll balance your glasses.

Said Vincent Van Gogh, "It's a blow,
Having two names-in-one, don't you know?
    It's just such a shock
    To be known as Van Gogh
By the Brits, while Yanks call me Van Gogh."

Cinderella's updated and hip.
Tradition's been given the slip.
    She thinks her Rolls nice,
    After pumpkin and mice -
And Buttons' replacement is Zip.

***

IV

CURSORY NURSERY

THREE blind mice, see how they all run:
They've a funny idea of what's fun.
The farmer's wild wife
Chased them all with a knife.
The *de-tails* that followed, I'll shun.

Old Mother Hubbard, who went to
The cupboard, was clearly intent to
Get a bone for the dog
And was plainly agog
At finding it bare: she'd not meant to.

Goldilocks' fame found its origin
In a house, while three bears were out forigin.
In their absence, it's said,
She used chairs, went to bed,
And emptied some bowls that had porigin.

The dish and the spoon had a row,
But the moon-jumping cow was a wow.
The little dog's glee
Came from neat lsd -
But he wasn't as high as the cow.

King's Men, who are unfeeling folk,
Made a fall guy of Humpty, poor bloke.
When he was dumped, he
Moaned, "Don't laugh at Humpty!"
But they howled: they could all see the yolk.

Cursory Nursery

. . . as high as the cow.

Cursory Nursery

A legendary lass called Miss Muffet
Was chased from her spider-prone tuffet.
    Next time, sad to say,
    That curds came her whey,
She curdseyed and told them to stuffet.

    Little Miss Muffet, they say,
    Used rather strong language the day
        A dirty great spider
        Sat down beside her:
    She curdsed it and then ran awhey.

Little Miss Muffet sat on a
Tuffet, but she was a goner:
    As soon as a spider
    Sat down beside her,
She got on her whey - did a runner.

***

Cursory Nursery

She curdsed it and then ran awhey

V

MUSICAL ITEMS

SAID a Sassenach trapped in Dunoon,
"The bagpipes are clearly a boon
For frightening hosts
Of goblins or ghosts.
What a pity there's only one tune."

Life was designed as an idyll
With a paradox right up the midyll.
But joy took a blow
(And a scrape and a bow):
Someone invented the fiddle.

Apologise, fiddlers! Escape
From involvement in musical rape!
You've shown you don't know
How to scrape with a bow -
So will you, overdue, bow and scrape?

When pop groups play live, go in dread:
The sounds will explode in your head.
Leather-lunged boys
Would make far less noise
If, just for a change, they'd play dead.

A young rock guitarist called Pete
Declared, "I'm admitting defeat.
I don't have the nous
To play Brahms or Strauss.
My Bach is much worse than my beat."

Musical Items

Bah-bah, beh-beh, bah-bah.
Means goodbye to baby - from Pa?
This cringe-making sound
Is now rarely around,
But gave us a bit of a jar.

Sopranos and tenors are prone
To sing a good tune on their own -
But choirs design
Contraltos a line
Which is murder when warbled alone.

When putting the choir through its paces,
The maestro said, "Don't lose your places.
The fact is, soprani
Sound ever so fani
When trying to sing like the basses."

The strangest of people by far
Are those of the genus Rock Star.
Though their aim is acclaim
And the favours of fame,
Dark glasses conceal who they are.

Said Beethoven, "People prefer
Their music to give them a stir.
A piece that will thrive
Is Symphony 5 -
The one that goes *d-d-d-der.*"

Any alto, of course, will know why
Her title can safely deny
The theory that Italy
Christened it wittily
(Since *alto* in Naples means *high*)*

*Except that *contra*, as in *contralto*, means *opposite of.*

Musical Items

Saying musical names isn't wise. It
Makes laughter whenever he tries it.
        No problem when WE say
        Chopin and Bizet -
But then he goes Shoppin' and Buys-it.

        The fellows who sing in a choir,
        And do as conductors desoir,
                Are tenors and basses
                Who take up their plasses
        With ladies who somehow sing hoir.

Though Mozart composed with a smile,
The effort became quite a trial,
        Until came the day
        When his death paved his way
To decompose just for a while.

VI

THE WORLD OF WORDS

A duchess who takes tea at Claridge's
Knows nothing of folk she disparages.
She wrote on her blotter,
"I think a train spotter
Is someone who makes acne carriages."

Rosaline was a young woman who,
When a word looked absurd, gave a clue.
When someone said, "Roz,
What on earth is a twos?"
She replied, "It's the plural of two."

MPs cry, *"'ear, 'ear!"* amid cheers.
They vote *Aye*, they vote *No*, it appears.
These things form the base
Of democracy's face:
The ayes and the noes and two ears.

The bell tolls for Greenland - oh, hell!
It tolls for Alaska as well.
It tolls for most places
With vast snowy places.
They say that it's Eskimo knell.

Bricklehampton deserves much more fame -
Not for its charms but its name.
A bit of a freak,
It may be unique:
All those letters and no two the same.

The World of Words

Among all life's urgent demands,
Who can tell me that he understands
What kind of an idjit'll
Chose the word *digital*
For a watch with no fingers or hands?

We're clearly all going insane,
But this is too soon to complain.
The crunch will come when.
In a roll-call of men,
Every Tom, Dick and Harry's called Wayne.

Jeune fille qui habite ã Rouen
Sees a ship with a colourful crouen,
On its way to Marseille
To steille for the deille.
It's because there's a naval revouen.

Guy is a word which once meant
A figure of fun - then it went
On to assail
Anybody who's male,
And it's right, to a certain extent.

There's only one right way to measure
The worth of that expert you treasure:
An ex, we have seen,
Is just a has-been,
And a spurt is a drip under pressure.

A TEN-WORD LIMERICK

Ambulatory craze,
Peripatetical daze.
Fairly immense
Directional sense:
Orienteers amaze.

The World of Words

It's clear, though it seems rather trite,
That Chinamen just don't ignite.
You rub them together
While finding out whether
Two Wongs really don't make a light.

Linguistics mean little to Bill.
"Buenos noces!" he murmurs in Lille.
"Por favor!" he will roar,
When lost in Lahore,
And *"Merci!"* when found in Seville.

No explanation is known,
To let a good reason be shown
Why rhymes for *brown, clown,*
Crown, drown, frown and *gown*
Disown *blown, flown, grown, mown* and *sown.*

Alphabetically speaking, you may
Be certain that *night* follows *day*;
That *spring* precedes *summer*
And *leak* precedes *plumber*,
And *grass* is what comes before *hay*.

A hidebound old chap from Braemar,
Who refused to refer to catarrh,
Declared, "It's not normal
To be so informal:
Ca-thankyou's more proper by far."

Farewell to our lbs and our ozs!
Brussels exlbs and pronozs.
Gramme, euro and litre
Will make our lives switre -
But not Eurocheque if it bozs.

The World of Words

Said a Pole to a Finn, "Don't demolish,
Or otherwise bruise or abolish,
    Or even diminish
    This pole's Finnish finish
By spoiling its posh Polish polish."

    Apostrophe's in the wrong place's
    Point finger's at teachings disgrace's.
        Uncertain user's
        Are loyal abuser's.
    (Plural's get one in all case's).

Italian food, one can show,
Where gender's concerned, is no go.
    Tagliatelle
    Does not fill the belle
And furnish a front that is beau.

    Labour or Liberal or Tory,
    We share the Remembrance Day story -
        Ubiquitous poppy,
        Lapel and jalopy -
    And sing *Land of Opium Glory.*

THE GAME OF THE NAME

To say Llan/fairpwllgwy/syllgo-
gerychwyrnd/robwllty/silio-
    gogogoch to the end
    Will largely depend
On not interrupting your flow.

Saying Llanfair in full is a deli-
cate task, and your tongue turns to jeli.
    Success is quite rare -
    And before you get there,
You may have to practise Pwllheli.

ENGLISH AS SHE IS BROKE

Luddites of language will say,
Excusing the havoc they play:
"We don't need forgiving!
Our English is living!"
(Despite being murdered each day).

Meet is a four-letter word
Whose meaning is clear, never blurred.
But an ignorant pup
Started saying *meet up.*
Meet up with then attained the absurd.

People who've never learned how
To use their own language allow
The spread of a crime
Called *This moment in time.*
The word that eludes them is *Now.*

Tautology's always the same:
Too many words in the frame.
What's nice and secure?
Safe haven, for sure.
A haven's exactly the same.

"Pre-conditions" are now in position:
Un-needed linguistic addition.
They're what you might state
Before you debate -
Rather like, as it were, a condition.

Forward planning's a trend which is lent
A mystique, to a certain extent
It got off the ground
Through a thinker who found
Little point when he planned post-event

"I've nothing to do!" said Fred's brother.
"Same goes for me", said his mother.
They've joined in a plan
Which means that they can
Have nothing to do with each other.

ONE OVER THE EIGHT

A Nine-Word Limerick

Environmentally tired!
Demonstrably under-inspired!
Intoxication!
Amelioration -
Opportunistic - required!

Invaded, he's apt to inveigh
Against those who invade to purvey
Their goods and pervade
Any place they invade.
They purveyed, he inveighed - Oh, I say!

THE ALPHABETICAL LIMERICK*

A bimbo can daily excite
Fat gentlemen ("Harry, invite
Jowly kittenish lot:
Men nurtured on pot;
Quite red skinned - though uptight, very white.")

** The challenge is open to you*
To follow this all the way through,
A to Z: we prepare
To meet (rather rare)
A Xanthian yellowing zoo.

William, a tar on a whaler,
Wore a glass in one eye without fail - a
Singular lens.
He was known to his friends
As Monocle Bill the Sailor.

Paradoxical language compounds
Sight and hearing: a cello astounds!
If I read it from books,
You will hear how it looks;
If I play it, you'll see how it sounds.

THE MONOSYLLIMERICK

A word game, a sort of a sport,
Is not to use long words but short.
No word must have two,
Still less boast a few -
You guess what - for a verse of this sort.

Aldwych tube station's procession
Of consonants - six in succession -
Is seen on its sign.
Thoughts on the same line
At Knightsbridge are given expression.

ONE UNDER THE EIGHT

A Seven-Word Limerick

Saying Llanfair/pwllgwy/syllgo-
gerychwyrnd/robwlly/silio-
gogogoch accidentally
Is fundamentally
Incomprehensible: No?

If Bangor were given a nought
Out of 10 in a damning report
Which called it "the end",
Would it thereby descend
To being the final resort?

The English knew what they were doing
With meanings for *killing* and *booing*.
They made it quite clear
There had to appear
A contrast with billing and cooing.

FIGURATIVELY SPEAKING

Fifty-four, one, five hundred **- you smiled**
At a game that's entirely compiled
With numerals numerous:
You thought it was humorous.
But then, you got LIVID - that's wild!

A hundred-and-one, six **and** ***fifty***
Take a long time to write. For the thrifty
Romans instead,
Like the tongue in their head,
It's CIVIL - their speed is quite nifty.

A thousand-and-nine, **with no tricks:**
A recipe easy to fix.
It just takes a trio
Of letters ***con brio:***
A perfectly straightforward MIX.

Lisped Sally, "I know I'm a dunth -
Yeth, I am, tho don't all thpeak at wonth -
But I think it'th abthurd
When they thay there'th no word
That rhymth at all nithely with *month*."

The World of Words

Short words with the ending *A-R*,
Like *bar, car, far, jar, mar* and *star,*
Have found rhyming strife
With *war* all their life:
Where war is concerned, strife is par.

The bellringer made no apologies,
Compiling appealing anthologies
In a bell tent with which
He achieved perfect pitch
On a site where he spent campanologies.

A high-speed young fellow from Brum
Would whiz back and forth with a chum.
They hurtled as one
From whither they'd gone,
Then tore back to whence they had come.

Cried the Wizard of Oz, "I denounce
The morons who all mispronounce
My name, adding weighting,
But minimal rating,
To me, as the Wizard of Ounce."

A helpful young fellow from Skye,
Whose zest for good causes ran high,
Would search for support,
With banners quite short:
"Dyslexsci, sit mite ot untie!"

Oh, Terry, Patricia, you're ratty! Oh,
Can't you accept that we're batty? Oh,
Don't get upset!
Just try to forget
We've nicknamed you Terrace and Patio.

If you look for a rhyme based on Tucson,
What a difficult task you're let lucson.
And *une jeune fille Francaise*
Vous regarde and then caise
That she thinks that it's all *très amucson*

SOMETHING BEGINNING WITH A

An actor, achieving an aim,
Accepts all applause and acclaim,
Astonishing any
At Abergavenny -
An audience always aflame.

AN E-LESS LIMERICK

This stanza has nothing which may
Prompt shock or a mild "Oh, I say!"
All that it's at
Is its plan to shun that
Non-consonant following *A*.

SOMETHING BEGINNING WITH A ... AND an E-less Limerick

Ask any artist around:
"Arty" acts always abound,
And allow any ass -
And "artist", alas -
Adulation as antics astound.

Coffee's the drink of today!
Cappucino, espresso - hurray!
In Spain, it was black,
But they've never looked back
Since someone found *café olé*

WELL, I'LL BE HANGED!

When Higgins (Professor) harangued*
Life's language-abusers, he clanged.
Those who murder their tongue,
He declaimed, should be hung.
Henry first - the fellow meant *hanged*.

Writing *hung*, meaning *hanged* - even though
It's required for a rhyme - is no go.
In a nice little earner
For Alan Jay Lerner,
Semantics produced their own Loewe.

It isn't too hard to discern a
Misuse of English to earn a
Sigh. But, my dears,
They've not used it for years
In America: this was a Lerner.

* It would have been apt to remind you of the well-known couplet concerned, but the original publisher of Lerner and Loewe's *My Fair Lady* in the United States refused permission.

A verse-writing fellow from Glos
Has worked out a rhyme for *Moss Bros*.
The trick up his sleeve
Is using abbrev,
Which helps him to make it all poss.

The World of Words

A musical man from the Hallé,
Who holiday-camped in a chalet,
Was asked if he'd been
In touch with Hugh Green.
He answered, "Hugh Green was my valet."

As a rule, it is quite fundamental
That a gunshot wound's most detrimental.
If a fellow went west
With a hole in his chest,
Would his death therefore be occidental?

A Lincolnshire lad saw the frost on
The form-filling folk he was lost on.
Asked "Born?", he said, "Born."
It took ages to dawn,
By *born*, he meant Bourne, near Boston.

Round about now should allow
Some questions to furrow the brow.
Few users could show
They actually know
Round what, about which and why now.

A bather named Mather would rather
Rhyme *lather* with *gather* than *father*.
He'll say that this verse
May well make him curse -
But deny he's in rather a lather.

Because there's no logical limiter
Keeping speech in a pleasing perimeter,
Fashion's barometer,
Which opts for ki*lo*metre,
Presumably blesses mil*li*metre.

The whole Parkhurst system was creaking.
Three inmates walked out, broadly speaking.
With haste but no tact,
The boss man was sacked*.
An escapegoat was what they were seeking.

* The escape of three Parkhurst prisoners in January 1995 brought to a head a general disenchantment with the prison service.

THE SELF-LINKED LIMERICK

. . . in which the last letter of each word is the same as the first letter of the next word; and the last letter of the last word is the same as the first letter of the first.

September, remember, returns,
Sublime every year; really yearns
Some extra applause -
Especially yours,
Suppressing gigantic concerns.

What meteorology lacks is
Some weather to prompt frantic faxes.
Nobody logs
When it rains cats and dogs -
But what if it starts hailing taxis?

A clock on its south elevation
Was seen as the first indication
That Pisa's famed tower
Could boast from that hour
Both the time and its known inclination.

The World of Words

Her is a word that is said
By Liverpool natives, instead
Of hair. I've inferred you
Discover that Urdu
Is something on top of your head.

WORDS

"Words", she averred, "are a bore.
I hate them each day more and more.
Their monitored meanings
And literary leanings
Are things that I simply deplore.

"Excitement would flow from the pen
If meanings were changed now and then:
If *green, hiccup, shrine*
Meant *seven, eight, nine,*
What pleasure to count up to ten!

"I'll explain my proposal like this:
Debenture dog wardrobe can bliss,
Charisma repent
Runs popular bent,
Berate a potato abyss."

Sewing's a craft that's so pure
That reasons grow steadily fewer
For a person who sews
To be likely in prose
To be just written off as a sewer.

The World of Words

The ship's barber's an affable nutter.
His customers stand back and mutter -
    But go on to savour
    His nautical flavour:
His shop's called the Clipper and Cutter.

    That tautologous form of attack,
    The head-butt, alas and alack,
        Can happen as quick
        As the well-known foot-kick,
    The fist-punch and of course the hand-smack.

Since home is the place you reside,
I quite understand, now I've tried,
    Why, if home's residential,
    It's quite evidential
You reside and reside 'til you've died.

    A barbecue seems to imply
    A wait for a haircut: that's why
        South Africans tend
        On the whole to depend,
    When cooking outside, on a *braai.*

A small boy in France may aver
That errors can sometimes occur.
    His mother's a mare,
    His father's a pear,
And his sister is always called Sir.

    English has nurtured within it
    The process for change to begin. It,
        Alas, as we know, meant
        It made *at the moment*
    The far less precise *at the minute.*

Supposing you die of starvation,
Whatever your gender or station,
You will know in advance,
If you do it in France,
Faim fatal is the true explanation.

IT WON'T WASH

Just why doesn't *wash* rhyme with *ash?*
It ought to go nicely with *bash*
(And *brash, cash, clash, crash,*
Dash, flash, gash, gnash, hash,
Lash, mash, rash, sash, slash, splash* and *trash).

There isn't an *A*, but an *O*,
In the words that *wash* rhymes with, and so
You soon get the hang:
Exclamations and slang -
***Bosh, dosh, gosh, nosh, posh, tosh* all flow.**

MPs who "make perfectly clear"
Are abusing the tongue we hold dear.
Their sheer obfuscation
Defies penetration:
It's clear it's not clear, nowhere near.

A lively young lady called Zoe,
Whose brother was Joe, said, "Althoe
Does not have a *Y*.
He is anxious to try,
In its absence, to call himself Joe."

A disconsolate lass, Freya Clare,
Announced, "My name makes me despair.
By baptismal mistake,
I sound like a cake
For which you don't pay - *free éclair.*"

FLOWERING DISCONTENT

An aubrieta* complained, "I'm a flower
That people misspell by the hour.
You'll usually see
An *I* after *T*
Before *A*, and it makes me quite sour."

***Aubrieta's* a name that we say**
In a highly illogical way.
The *eesh*, to be fair,
Just shouldn't be there:
No *I* after *T* before *A*.

**Collins Guide to Alpines & Rock Gardens* (1985 edition) listed "Aubrieta (often spelt aubrietia)." How right it was: *The New Collins Concise Dictionary* (1985 edition) was in the *aubrietia* school.

But *The Flower Expert*, by Dr D G Hessayon (1984) , *The Reader's Digest Encylopaedia of Garden Plants and Flowers* (1985) and *The Royal Horticultural Society Gardeners' Encylopedia of Plants and Flowers* (1989) are among the gardening books saying *aubrieta* without equivocation and quite possibly knowing what they are talking about - even if two of them cannot agree on *encyclopaedia* or *encyclopedia.*

There are loonies at large who could harm a
Language that's always a charmer;
Who, saying they think
That it's rude to say *Chink*
(Meaning Chinese), ban *chink* in the armour.

Freya Rose sighed, "They imparted
A name to dismay the half-hearted.
You can see how it goes:
Freya Rose, fray arose,
War began, or at least, battle started."

OUT OF THE RECKONING

A collector of oddities thundered,
"Though it's something you may not have wondered,
If you DO want to say
Lots of words without *a*,
You can just count from one to one hundred."

(From the counting, it ought to be said
That ten other letters have fled:
In addition to *a*,
Where are *b, c, j, k,*
l, m, p, q, w, z?)

SCISSORS

A dazed etymologist said,
"I cannot get out of my head
That of the four esses
That *scissors* possesses,
Three are pronounced like a Z."

American experts could see
They could do little else but agree -
Recognition which led
To footnotes which said,
"Although he said Z, he meant Z."

Has anyone here understood
Why *blood* is quite clearly no good
For rhyming with *brood*,
Edwin Drood, food, mood, rood,
Not to mention *hood, stood, good* and *wood?*

NOTHING DOING

Limericks deter infiltration
By words of great length and duration
That's why they've stayed free
Of *floccinauci-*
***nihilipilification**.**

The limerick's space, shape and duration
Limit word utilisation.
What room could there be
For *floccinauci-*
nihilipilification?

* The action or habit of estimating as worthless.

On the Isle of Capri, where Frank drank,
He was given great status and rank.
He stood out a mile:
He was not rank-and-file -
He was one on his own, Island Frank.

Laisser faire is a term I have known
For many a year. I have grown
To be so aware
Of the joy of *don't care*,
That now I can't leave it alone.

Said a poet who came from Madras,
"My writing in English is crass.
I have studied the rules
Of the poetry schools,
And I can't rhyme *was, has* and *alas*."

A LIE-LOW LIMERICK

**Limericks lurk undetected,
Unnoticed, unseen and protected -
But isn't it strange
That *Home on the Range*
Should have one that no-one's suspected?**

**Four-fifths of a limerick lay
Where the deer and the antelope play,
(Where there's never been heard
A discouraging word,
And the skies are not cloudy or grey).**

It's good that two lords could agree
On what each one's interest should be.
We'd not like a language
That bet on the Sandwich
And had plum jam derbies for tea.

Well, basically's phrasing we bring
To deal with a question: we cling
To tradition that's been
Overused. What's it mean?
Well, basically, not a damn' thing.

Does anyone else wonder when
There will be an awareness in men
That they really should try
Minuscule with one *I*,
And *restaurateur* with no *N?*

A fire and a saddle complete
A pairing where opposites meet.
The saddle, of course,
Is the seat of the horse.
The fire is the source of the heat.

MY WORD

Lexicographers, as they reflect
The changes in language, elect
To condone the abusage
In ignorant usage
Of the gem they are there to protect.

Lexicographers no longer try
Protecting our language. That's why
They imply they concur
That we're free to infer
That *infer* means the same as *imply.**

Lexicographers clearly aren't bright.
They go with the flow, day and night.
The way their game's played is,
If we all thump old ladies,
Then thumping old ladies is right.

* This was a gem which emerged in a 1997 dictionary. Destruction continued in 1999, when it was decided that *disinterested* now means the same as *uninterested.*

A FIVE-WORD LIMERICK

Llanfair/pwllgwy/syllgo-
gerychwyrnd/robwlly/silio-
gogogoch represents
A/manuens-
es' unforgettable flow.

Paddle your own canoe,
A phrase that is well-known to you,
        Puzzles Frenchmen who may
        Think they're hearing you say,
Pas de lieu Rhône que nous.

ON THE MOVE

***Going head over heels,* it's been found,**
Is a good way of getting around.
        So we go everywhere
        With our heads in the air,
And our heels just below, on the ground.

***Getting down on all fours* is one more**
Sort of nonsense we ought to ignore,
        Since everyone sees
        Two hands and two knees
Are the four that we've got - just one four.

***Best foot forward,* it's easy to see,**
Grammatically speaking, can't be:
        What a challenge to beat!
        An impossible feat -
Unless, that's to say, you've got three.

There's a lady who calls herself Mrs,
Who likes to be liberal with krs.
        "If I were a Ms,
        There'd be less of a bs -
But thrs what blrs", she hrs.

By and large, it just comes with our genes.
By and large, it is English that's Queen's.
        Preposition, conjunction
        And adjective function -
By what? What's so big? And it means. . ?

VII

ANARCHIC ANAGRAMS

WOODY ALLEN'S the name that you need
To create *A lewd loony*. Proceed:
David Mellor, by gad,
Makes *Dim lover lad.*
Erode liver? That's Oliver Reed.

"Graham Taylor* for England!" they cried.
But World Cup hopes stuttered and died.
The team took a toss
And so did the boss.
Ah, goal martyr! They howled for his hide.

* Graham Taylor lost his job as manager of the England football team in 1991.

Slap-happy Stanley adores
The season of goodwill because,
Well mellow and blotto,
He sits in a grotto:
Casual Stan's Santa Claus.

Letters unite, side by side,
Forming words like *United*; divide
Those letters and start
Watching words fall apart:
United quite soon is untied.

Elvis died and then sightings occurred.
"The King is alive!" was the word.
Elvis shuffles and gives
The anagram *lives* -
Which helps to explain what we heard.

MAN DOWN THE PAN

T S Eliot soon started to give a damn,
The day that it dawned that his dad and mam
Had not seen at the font
That their son would not want
***Toilets* upheld as his anagram.**

When DID T S Eliot find
That his name was becoming a bind?
When he wrote it one day
And found with dismay
That *toilets* were coming to mind.

England lost lots of tests in a row.
National pride took a hell of a blow.
The captain resigned -
And Gooch*, you will find,
Is easily turned to *Och, go!*

* Graham Gooch gave up the captaincy of England's Test team in 1991.

A word to the wise: there's a chance a
Word to the wise may enhance a
Sensation of sighs:
A *word* to the *wise*
Brings widowers up as the answer.

Anarchic Anagrams

Delia Smith is a name that reveals
The secret few knew it conceals.
Something was cooking
When no-one was looking.
So what did it hide? *It hid meals!*

Paul Gascoigne*, turned about face,
Emerges as *Sing up, goal ace!*
But Gazza slipped up
(O, leg saga in Cup!)
And what about *Goal, using pace?*

Paul Gascoigne's post-Wembley reward -
A whacking great transfer abroad -
Was earlier showing
In *Cup! A sale! Going!*
In his name, his career had been stored.

* This controversial soccer star, who suffered a severe leg injury in the 1991 FA Cup Final, also sang on a quickly-forgotten record. When he recovered from his injury, he was transferred to an Italian club.

Although she quite failed to disarm a
Threat that was going to harm her,
Margaret Thatcher could claim
That under her name,
She always remained *The Great Charmer*

Las Vegas is where the *lass gave*
Last buck (fortune favours the brave)
She salvages what
She can: not a lot.
Las Vegas has won - so *Sag, slave!*

Though a lout is a pain, let's enjoy
This truth: uncouth youth is a toy
Of a language which shows
How clearly it knows
That a yob is a poor backward *boy.*

HAVE AN ICE DAY

Nancy Kerrigan* suffered a jar
In an infamous effort to mar
Her hopes. *N K ran*
***Icy anger:* a man**
Thumped her hard on the knee with a bar.

The Kerrigan name's on a slice
Of silver for skating on ice -
But it changed at one stage
Into world-wide *rink rage.*
They had clobbered young Nancy. Not nice!

* American ice skater who won a silver medal in the 1994 Winter Olympics in Norway after being attacked by a supporter of one of her opponents in an effort to put her out of contention.

The rhyme is a crime, but the plot
Of *A novel* - read on! - *by a Scott-*
ish writer will show,
When transposed, *Ivanhoe,*
By Sir ("Make me scan!") *Walter Scott.*

THIRTEEN

***Twelve plus one* is an anagram: who**
Could have thought what some tweaking might do?
Yet a curious mind
Has managed to find
That it hides in *Eleven plus two.*

Anarchic Anagrams

The thought of a privileged school
Makes the Left's hackles rise as a rule.
        But then Tony Blair*
        Showed Conservative flair:
As *Tory in Lab*, he's no fool.

* Soon after becoming leader of Britain's Labour Party in 1994, Tony Blair hit the headlines with his decision to send his son to a grant-maintained school. His policies, after he became Prime Minister in May 1997, led *The Independent* to describe him before the end of the year as being "on a mission driven by Thatcherite zeal."

Cremation is over and done.
The wake, thank the Lord, has begun.
        Another poor bloke
        Has gone up in smoke:
His funeral's become *real fun.*

Anagrams, caught in the raw,
Should be relevant: that's what they're for!
        Schoolmaster is where?
        In *the classroom*, so there!
Woman Hitler is *mother-in-law.*

***

VIII

IMPERFECTLY CORRECT

SAID a student of language in Bray,
"The people who call themselves gay
Should instead introduce
For their personal use
Gay that's spelled *gey*, as in fey."

Alternative funny men say
There's a code it's correct to obey.
The things they can choose,
They abuse to amuse
(In a vulgar but quite correct way).

THE CHAIR

The "politically right" strangely swear
That a head of committee's a chair!
They've all failed to spot
That most chairs have got
Four legs, which are quite often square.

That very strange person, The Chair,
Found people were starting to stare:
In charge at a meeting,
Was rapidly bleating,
When pulled up and sat on four-square.

Imperfectly Correct

*Themself** is an ace in the hand
Of those by whom gender is banned -
A singular plural
And culpable cure-all
Where *himself* or *herself* should stand.

* Birmingham City Council officials ordered that *themself* should be used on 1994 Care Week posters so that they read, *Do you care for someone who is unable to look after themself?*

Handyperson required. What a joke!
So correct - but they wanted a bloke.
So the person who came,
With her five-foot-one frame,
Found she had to start felling an oak.

THE STATUS DEBATE

Said a forceful young woman from Bicester
(So forceful that none could resicester):
"I'm not Miss or Mrs.
I'm Ms because thrs
Like letting a man cut short Micester."

She explained that by being a Ms
She was giving herself quite a bs.
"I've hidden my status
Behind just two latus -
The same as a mere Mr ds.

"When a woman is labelled a Mrs,
She finds she can miss out on krs
She'd otherwise get
When a man wants to pet.
"Thrs so silly!" she hrs.

MAN MANAGEMENT

Man is a word being banned,
But the normal huperson can't stand
Personiacal folk
Who personage to choke
If a woperson's not the top hand.

The loonies' *man* madness will worsen -
They'll all fall to spitt'n and curs'n -
When dawns the great shame
Of Labour's own name,
Wrapped around able-bodied seaperson.

THE FREAKS HAVE A WORD FOR IT

The antics of cranks cannot charm a
Student of English who's calmer.
They seek to declare
That a *nip in the air*
Should be banned, with *a chink in the armour.*

Their lunacies now stretch so far,
If you call a sheep black, they go *"Bah!"*
Since it's also not right
For a sheep to be white,
What colourless bleaters they are!

With coffee, they're fearless and frank:
Look for sense, and you'll just draw a blank.
So it's *with* or *without* -
And they don't talk about
What they like to be in at the bank.

Black people, of course, say they're black. . .

Black people, of course, say they're black -
The word which takes oddballs aback.
Yet careful inspections
Of mirrored reflections
Could hint that they're on the right track.

ME

When do people first make the absurd
Decision that *me's* a rude word?
Such thoughts must be why
Between you and I
Is ever-increasingly heard.

To what can their blind spot be due,
This huge non-accusative crew?
Between you and I
Is their cry 'til they die,
But they'd run from *between I and you.*

JUST ABOUT THE STRENGTH OF IT

A he-man complained, "There will be
Political problems for me.
I rather suspect
I won't be correct
If I'm not person-person, you see."

But wait: *person* very well might
Hurt those for whom gender's a slight.
Sons and daughters are *kin*:
Though the he-man might grin,
***Perkin-perkin* is just about right.**

Imperfectly Correct

It’s easy to see in a trice
That the meaning of *Vice Chair’s* precise:
        It’s the chair where you sit
        While enjoying a bit
Of behaviour that’s naughty but nice.

IX

A SLIP OF THE TONGUE

WITH six Swiss wrist watches, the trick
Is knowing which wrist watch to nick.
If you make a botch,
Your neighbourhood watch
Won't think that you got one on tick.

With most fish, I've no wish to feel pally but
There is one which will cause me to dally but
I have to be sure
It's clever and pure:
A celibate cerebral halibut.

She started to say, for a joke,
"The bloke's black bike's back brake block broke.
The sixth sheikh's sixth sheep
Is sick and asleep."
You could see she was sorry she spoke.

I think you may finally flip
If ever you try to let rip:
Gig whip gig whip gig!
Whip gig - make it big! -
Gig whip! Gig whip gig! Whip gig whip!

A Slip of the Tongue

Your tongue may well take some unkinking

A Slip of the Tongue

Although you can say, *Still the sinking*
Steamer sank, without possibly thinking
    That you might well be sorry -
    Red lorry, red lorry -
Your tongue may well take some unkinking.

X

REVERSALS

It's a curse! Let's rehearse, to explore
How the world in reverse is a chore.
Imagine things stay
Dyslexia's way:
front-to-back lines the all seeing You're.

*

A dyslexic agnostic called Hogg
Never managed to sleep like a log.
He'd get into states
In his small-hours debates,
And he'd doubt the existence of doG.

Rotavator's a word that can cater
For folk who reverse visual data.
Rot comes before
A-V-A and then *tor,*
And backwards it spells *rotavatoR.*

Able was I ere I saw
Elba. Yes, that was before
The reversible state
Of his back-and-forth fate
Brought him fame - what's his name? - ever more.

Drawer rotavator reward
Is something to play with if bored.
No need to rehearse
To write in reverse:
It has palindromic accord.

Reversals

Getting words back-to-front is a chore
For a fellow who lives on the moor:
    When in a dab doom,
    Thinks the moor is a room,
And worries about Cromwell's straw.

    A phonetics fanatic called Sydney,
    Who'd had renal failure in Lydney,
        Said, "The sign in reverse
        Could not have been worse:
    Indicator reversed's *rot-a-kidney*."

Said Naomi, "Though I have grown
To be a young girl who is known
    To be happy and gay
    When things go my way,
A reversal's result is *I moan*."

XI

OLD HAROLD

OLD Harold believes Joan of Arc
Was a lady who chose to embark
    With Noah in a boat
    In which they could float.
As to why, he's a bit in the dark.

    Old Harold believes opera's need,
    When filling a drama-charged lead,
        Is a man with the knack,
        When stabbed in the back,
    Not to carry on singing but bleed.

Old Harold surprised an old flame
With his socks like a pantomime dame:
    One black and one white,
    But he said, "It's all right -
There's a pair in the house, just the same."

    Old Harold was out with the boys,
    Tickling trout, which he always enjoys,
        When the keeper, O'Dowd,
        Cried, "No fishing allowed!"
    He whispered, "Who's making a noise?"

Old Harold says joy is complete:
He's sorted out parking a treat.
    He's found that most places
    Have hundreds of spaces
On yellow lines all up the street.

Old Harold

Old Harold says bathrooms can't beat
Equipment with no wooden seat -
Just taps for revising
How high a jet's rising.
It's lovely for washing your feet.

Old Harold had finished his chore,
With the jigsaw complete on the floor.
He explained, amid cheers,
"The box said *Five years,*
But I have just done it in four."

Old Harold's a bit of a mutt.
His joy in a car wash goes *phut*!,
When he's sitting in there,
Sort of wet and aware
That none of his windows is shut.

Old Harold's a devil for whist:
Though you don't want to play, he'll insist.
But it goes on so late,
With his endless debate
On whether to stick or to twist.

***

XII

LOGICAL LAPSES

SAID a fellow from Leamington Spa
Who fitted square wheels on his car:
"After shopping around,
They're the best things I've found
To ensure that the potholes don't jar."

Intelligent sailors like me
Bore holes in their boats - two or three -
So that when they go down
They're not likely to drown,
Ten miles from land, out at sea.

A far-sighted Boeing mechanic
Torched the plane with a grin that was manic.
He said, "I have found
If it burns on the ground,
We're all far less likely to panic."

A wise old owl who was asked why
He'd plucked out his feathers said, "I
Am avoiding the jolt
That I'll get if I moult
And drop like a bolt from the sky."

An amateur gardening nut
Sprayed his lawn with a hose from a butt.
It was not H-two-O:
It was scrumpy, and so
It ensured that the grass came half-cut.

Logical Lapses

A wine connoisseur, name of Plunkett,
With a task to complete, didn't funk it.
He smashed up his cellar,
This thoughtful old feller,
To avoid being sad when he'd drunk it.

"Why is this called a boom, Uncle Fred?"
Asked a young tyro sailor named Ted.
He now knows, we assume:
We all heard it go *boom*!
When it thumped on the back of Ted's head.

Newton's Law soon ensured its longevity -
Its apple-borne option was brevity -
When he chose to behave
In a way that was grave,
Which means that there's no Law of Levity.

When a watch doesn't work, that's OK:
It's useful to keep it that way.
Unlike those that go,
But run fast or slow,
It tells the right time twice a day.

Though time may stand still or go fast,
We know its condition won't last.
If now, by rehearsing,
We start it reversing,
Our future will be in the past.

A parachute jumper from Fife
Said, "Boredom, alas, is quite rife.
The time that is stored
For pulling the cord
Is always the rest of my life."

Logical Lapses

I've heard fish described as a dish
That's good for the brain - so I wish
Somebody would try
Explaining just why
Fish are stupid, though totally fish.

How can every Jumbo defy
All gravity's laws in the sky?
With all that dead weight,
And humans and freight,
What idiot thought it might fly?

As we know flight recorders stand shocks
Like explosions and crashing on rocks,
Is it just by mistake
We don't manage to make
An aircraft as strong as its box?

Some women, though oddly at ease
When hemlines rise high above knees,
Exposing the thighs
That bring tears to your eyes,
Are appalled to be called just a tease.

The gas board's researchers were bright.
Their research was resourceful and right.
But they reached an *impasse*
With their new safety gas:
It was safe, but it wouldn't ignite.

A horse-loving laddie called Keith
Upset the good burghers of Leith.
He guessed all their ages,
But did it in stages,
Insisting on counting their teeth.

When a watch had two hands, there occurred
Something odd - though you've probably heard.
To the hour hand (quite cute)
And the minute (minute)
Came a new second hand as a third.

With a diet, the whole situation
Needs willpower and great concentration.
When any food's near,
Your response must be clear:
Eat the lot and remove the temptation.

MILLENNIUM MISCOUNT

New Year's Eve '99, the world thought,
Was millennium's end - a year short,
And a stance quite absurd,
From which we inferred
That the first year AD was year nought.

If the first year AD was year none,
And the next year AD was year one,
Then everything's fine
And so '99
Could have seen the millennium gone.

The wind, though it's here such a lot,
Presumably starts from some spot.
Has anyone found
A square yard of ground
Where it is, next to one where it's not?

Corn flakes are odd - they're reviewing 'em.
Nobody owns up to chewing 'em -
But they get in your teeth,
Both above and beneath:
The next move, perhaps, could be stewing 'em.

XIII

SIGNS OF UNCERTAINTY

ZIMMER *frei* are the words on display
In Austrian windows today.
Dismiss any claims
That they mean walking frames
Can be used with no charges to pay.

A fruit-picker, down on all-fours,
Told a farmer he met on the moors:
"Pick Your Own, says your sign -
But I've none to call mine,
Which is why I've come here, to pick yours."

A strawberry-picker said, "Please!"
To the farmer, from down on his knees.
"You say *Pick Your Own*:
I thought you'd have known,
As I've none of my own, I've picked these."

"Unauthorised access", signs say,
"Cannot be permitted." OK:
The ones that I've seen
Presumably mean
You may only come in if you may.

Licensed's the word that's the biz
For putting one into a tiz.
As signboards will tell,
It's the word one can't spell -
The more so, supposing one is.

Signs of Uncertainty

Sale signs could well prove to be sprats
Catching mackerels refurbishing flats.
Don't be seduced
By *"Carpets Reduced!"*
They may have reduced them to mats.

"This door is alarmed!" But what for?
If it's frightened to death, then there's more.
When it's frightened to death,
Death has claimed its last breath.
Its users thus stand at death's door.

"Plant ties", said the placard. Fred glowered.
The garden supplies man just cowered,
While Fred said, "Look here,
I did that last year.
My favourite tie never flowered."

Gasped a fly to his friend, "I won't stop
This circular sprint 'til I drop.
I've flown from afar
To land on this jar,
But the label says, *'Tear round the top.'*"

A tourist in Wales murmured, "Cor!
These place names are really a chore!
But some I can say
In my anglicised way -
And top of my list's Dolgellau."

A workman who came from Dunbar
Wrote words on the road like a star.
But the stencil he used
Left drivers confused:
Back-to-front, upside-down, it said *TLAH.*

Signs of Uncertainty

Presumably, part of the charm
Of a *"wireless* intruder alarm"*
Is to frighten the hound
Who is poking around
In the radio, doing it harm.

* *Wireless* is increasingly used in the sense of *without wires* - which clearly means that what was once a transistor radio is now a wireless radio, although nobody seems to have said so yet.

"Gigantic Boot Sale" means we'll meet
Great bargains we'll never repeat.
Each car is a stall
With goodies for all -
Not just those who have very large feet.

"Armitage Shanks" - it's quite true:
The headline looms large in the loo.
To be perfectly frank,
I don't know how to shank:
Did Armitage learn it from you?

A lovely young lady called Sue
Pinned a note on her door in full view:
"In the bath, please come in."
It made everyone grin,
But was meant for the man from the Pru.

An obedient fellow called Clive,
At a Guy Fawkes' Night party, said, "I've
Seen rules which require,
'Light fuse and retire' -
Which is great, as I'm just thirty-five."

Signs of Uncertainty

"Fast food", said the sign. Fred's aghast
At the awfulness of the repast.
        He's sure the sign meant
        That the food would prevent
All regrets about having to fast.

XIV

JUST BACK IN TIME

WILLIAM TELL made the onlookers gape
When all that misfired was their jape.
Tell didn't tell
That he shot very well,
So his son had an arrow escape.

J Caesar would never agree
That he came into Britain BC.
So by a decree
Made the other JC
AM 55 ("After Me.")

Cleopatra said, "Once in a while,
Dis Antony talk make me smile.
Yo may wonder why
Ah says it's a lie:
It's 'cos Ah'm de Queen of Denial."

An historian visiting Troy
Said, "It's just like I dreamed as a boy.
I entered, of course,
In a large wooden horse:
That's a ploy any boy would enjoy."

In spite of his governess-aunt,
Who told him, "You cannot! You shan't!",
Canute, silly man,
Known thus far as Can,
Played the waves and was soon known as Can't.

Just Back in Time

Said a fellow named Fawkes, "This is why
I spend every day on a high.
With gunpowder schemes
And impossible dreams,
I'm in love with a wonderful Guy."

A rus who was named after Ic
Must have felt quite decidedly sic -
Up there near the sun,
Wax starting to run
And feathers refusing to stic.

In the dungeons, a peasant from Bradley,
Who was there for behaving quite badly,
Assured every visitor,
"I'm told the Inquisitor
Has said he will stretch a point gladly."

Nobody doubted the mission
Or role of the great Inquisition.
You knew there'd be torture
If ever it corture:
It kindly explained your position.

In the bath, Archimedes knew why the
Level of water grew high. The
Result was a streaker
Whose cry of *"Eureka!"*
Made his wife say, "You smell not good either."

George Washington said, "I can't see
That the world wants descendants of me."
So without more ado,
And out of the blue,
He cut down his family tree.

Just Back in Time

". . . not at this dist. . ."

Just Back in Time

General Sedgewick was sadly not missed,
The day he stood up to insist
    That he wouldn't get shot
    And said, "They could not
Hit an elephant - not at this dist. . ."

    King Harold's last words, so they say,
    At the Battle of Hastings that day,
        Were, sadly, "I spy,
        With my little eye,
    Something beginning with *A*."

William Tell's son said, "I smell like this,
Because of attaining the heights of bliss.
    It's the way I behave
    When I've had a close shave.
You can put it all down to my Aramis."

    William Tell used to get in a stew,
    Encountering somebody new.
        When asked for his name,
        It was always the same:
    "Will Tell" brought the answer, "Please do."

King Harold, a barrel of woes,
Was offered advice by his foes.
    "You've only been shot:
    Try blinking a lot.
And what about blowing your nose?"

    Cried Canute, with his toes in the brine,
    "This identity crisis of mine:
        Should I stick to my notion
        And push back the ocean,
    Or turn the whole lot into wine?"

Just Back in Time

King Alfred tried hard to create
A cake on the hearth. Alas, Fate
Just burned up his bun
And left him with none,
And that's why he's Alfred the Grate.

Fame is elusive: expect it
To avoid those who try to collect it.
Too many were sure
Their place was secure -
But they then wrote their memoirs and wrecked it.

Said Henry VIII, "I declare",
As he helped a doomed wife to prepare
To meet her sharp fate,
"That I'm Head of State -
But I do like to carry a spare."

***

XV

LIFE ON THE LAND

A cow is in calf - but for now,
The question to answer is how
Farmers expect
The world to detect
That this means a calf is in cow.

Eggs haven't been square, said old Porter,
Since the good Lord decided he oughter
Give hens eyes so small
They were never at all
Quite able to squint or to water.

A farm student down in Torbay
Said, "An average, I think we can say,
Is something on which
Unless there's a hitch,
A hen lays an egg every day."

Hill farmers, it's easy to tell,
Are those who perhaps for a spell,'
Display health defects:
Hagricultural hex-
perts who just hain't very well.

While weeding, perspiring, Anstruther
Remarked to his soil-grubbing brother,
"Shifting docks, I depend
On pulling one end,
While the world's hanging on to the other."

Life on the Land

A gardening novice in Ware
Spreads, with techniques which are rare,
Botanical terror.
It's trowel and error:
Doesn't know, doesn't learn, doesn't care.

Sheepdogs in trials induce sleep:
They run and they crouch and they creep.
More skilled and inviting,
Amusing, exciting,
To do without dogs and train sheep.

A gardening expert called Tranter
Said, "Fezzes, inverted instanter,
When taken off craniums,
Look good with geraniums,
If ever you're short of a planter."

A wise poultry farmer said, "When
Electricity fails, it is then
That I show great resource -
Proceeding, of course,
To bring in a battery hen."

Some battery hens in Kings Lynn
Had hardly a chance to begin.
The farmer, the clot
Killed the whole broody lot
While putting the batteries in.

Said the herdsman, "I've been born and bred
To the job, but what fills me with dread
Is that one of these days,
When deserving of praise,
I'll just get a pat on the head."

Life on the Land

Britons abroad in their flats
Thought farmers back home must be rats
        When they learned that the fields
        Were giving good yields
From manure mostly made of expats.

        While up to his knees in the mire,
        Farmer Giles said, “I do not desire
                A red sky at night.
                It’s not shepherds’ delight:
        It just means the barn is on fire.”

XVI

RELIGIOUS DISORDERS

HELL'S taking a long time to burn! Oh,
The sinners are waiting their turn! Oh,
They want the quick thrill
Of a high-level grill -
Not Dante's *andante Inferno.*

In Sheffield, the Reverend Brain* gave
Voice to a bit of a brainwave.
"I'll dance like a dervish
At nine o'clock service,
And say that I'm having a Brain rave."

* The Rev Chris Brain, of St Thomas' Church, Sheffield, caused consternation in the Church of England with the revelation in 1995 of his regular disco-style services where bikini-clad girls "explored their sensuality" and Big Mac hamburgers featured in Holy Communion.

ROMAN AW, GEE!

The Catholic Church does have a slight
Piece of liturgical blight;
Tautological, too:
And also with you.
Ah, well! English wrong, Roman rite.

All glory and honour is yours
Gnaws the vitals and draws no applause.
Two subjects with *is*
Are pretty bad biz -
And time goes on sealing the flaws.

Religious Disorders

The bishop, the wicked old blighter,
Turns people first pale and then whiter.
    Disrobing reveals,
    To horrified squeals,
His head's the same shape as his mitre.

A man looked a bit of a freak
With his hat on in church, Sunday week.
    When a woman called Pat
    Said, "You're wearing your hat!",
He explained, "I like people to speak."

Prayer is a thing that's been hit
By experts in that which is fit.
    It's really quite odd
    To talk of a God
Who isn't a He, She or It.*

* The Church of England General Synod decided in July 1994 to rewrite prayers and services and make them more acceptable to feminists by removing references to gender as far as possible.

"Religion's decidedly odd.
It rules with the cruellest rod.
    Men kill and men maim,
    And it's all in its name.
Perhaps I should leave", murmured God.

A divinity student said he
Would never accept his degree.
    "Squeeze a camel", said Tweedle,
    "Through eye of a needle:
I still won't be Tweedle DD."

Religious Disorders

An old Trappist monk took a chance - a
Decision to speak, to advance a
More sociable day
But backed out half way:
When he talks to himself, there's no answer.

The Pope said, "I could be a slob,
Or a yob who belongs to The Mob.
I'd still be infallible,
Completely non-malleable:
It's one of the perks of the job."

The primate, the faithful could see,
Was cross with Creation as he
Played swings in a tyre
And asked with great ire,
"So who's made a monkey of me?"

An innocent novice called Clare
Was plagued by the Devil at prayer.
This caused her emotions
Which wrecked her devotions
And made Reverend Mother despair.

There's a problem at church: they're reviewing it.
They say that they'll soon be pursuing it.
From the time you go in,
They talk about sin,
But never quite get round to doing it.

Said a novice, "Life's fun, in the main -
And that's why religion's a strain.
When I'm tempted to stray,
I confess the next day -
And the next day, I'm straying again."

Religious Disorders

A cleric who'd strayed heard confession
For a man with two wives, and the session
Was brought to an end
When he told him, "My friend,
I've a similar silly obsession."

The Church's particular patter
On an old agricultural matter
Makes farming sound fun:
Rotavate it and run -
ie, plough the fields and scatter.

Said a lover of language called Rory,
"Though the Lord's Prayer's a beautiful story,
We'd improve it by far
If we muttered *"Thine ARE*
The kingdom, the power and the glory."

LET'S HEAR IT FOR HYMN

Singing praises, O Lord, in full flow
From a hymn sheet, is joyful - although
That joy is constrained,
Since no-one's explained
Why we can't have a lower case *o*

Said the Lord, "Let us not buck the trends
Every hymnal and hymn sheet extends:
Let's make it official.
To use My initial.
(I've always been O to My friends)."

A kindly young curate called Walter
Held an Easter Day service in Malta.
Curiosity burned,
Once locals had learned
Mrs Jones laid an egg on the altar.

XVII

ONE FOR THE ROAD

THE motor car serves as a cloak
For Britons whose brains are a joke.
Intelligence tests
Would sort out these pests
And clear all our roads at a stroke.

With lanes marked for traffic, the growth
Of stupid, undisciplined sloth
Is really a pain:
With more than one lane,
The norm is to straddle them both.

The front of a queue at a light
Is reserved for the not very bright.
It's only on green
That he lets it be seen
That he wants - blast the man! - to turn right.

On a winding road, chances are few
To overtake, but it is true
That while you don't dare,
The slowest car there
Always gets to the front of the queue.

A native of Southern Lahore
Pitched tent on the westbound M4.
Though Truman Capote
Ran over his dhoti,
He said he liked life in the roar.

One for the Road

People agree without question:
Cars simply cause more congestion.
So will they agree
To sink them at sea?
(The thought is called auto-suggestion).

Pedestrian precincts don't fuss:
They keep out all cars - but you cuss
When you walk and you find
That you're barged from behind
By a large and allowable bus.

"Catalytic converters for me!"
Cried the Reverend Paddy M'Gee.
"A converter - Oi ratalyt -
Converts a good catalyt
To an awfully good C of E."

A copper from old Wogga Wogga
Has a new radar gun as a logger.
Alas, what he clocks is
Four telephone boxes,
Three bus stops, two pubs and a jogger.

If you drink when you're driving, you've built
A setting for anger and guilt.
It's stupid and risky:
Beer, gin and whisky
Will mess up the car if they're spilt.

Your most vital needs when embarking
On bravely illegally parking
Are hazard lights, so
Everybody will know
And the Law simply can't help remarking.

One for the Road

A motor you cannot rely on
Is a bit of a gamble to try on
    A motorway - though,
    If it breaks down, you know
You'll have a hard shoulder to cry on.

In Boston, the burghers saw stars:
Car parks were talked of in bars.
    The new high-rise maze
    Was closed within days:
The plans hadn't counted on cars.*

* One car park was designed without allowing for the weight of the cars. Now strengthened and functional, it is always pointed out by drivers of Boston's tourist trolleys.

A lady in 'Frisco near died
With the joy of a cable car ride.
    The hills, seat and trolley
    Made things really jolly,
And she'd slide to the guy at her side.

Some deep-seated psyche explains
Why a motorway driver disdains,
    From Glasgow to Ipswich,
    To look for his dip switch -
And simply can't find inside lanes.

"But officer, this is a drag!"
"I know, sir, but don't lose your rag.
    You're nicked for the reason
    That this is the season
Of goodwill-and-blow-in-the bag."

One for the Road

A car driver's lack of regard
For place names made journeys ill-starred.
When lost near Reading,
He said he was heading
For Burnt. No-one guessed he meant Chard.

An indignant car driver from Dover
Was cross when police pulled him over.
They said, "Is that not
A dog licence you've got?"
He explained that his car was called Rover.

The sensible motorist has
Good maps, without fuss or pezazz.
They're usually said
To be A to Z,
But actually call themselves *AZ**.

* It's perfectly true: take a look at the front cover.

Those motorway drivers from hell
Who don't use their brains very well,
Form a queue in the main
In the packed centre lane,
While the inside's as clear as a bell.

God forbid we should sound too progressive -
But with morons in cars so aggressive,
If we used just one height
For front bumpers, we might
Make head-ons a bit less impressive.

Parking is always a fiddle,
With rules it's expensive to diddle.
To escape heavy fines,
Fred avoids yellow lines:
He parks in the street - up the middle.

One for the Road

Since phones first went mobile, they've shown
The dangers, not hitherto known,
        That we now have to meet
        Every day on the street
From the cars with a fool on the phone.

        Motorway morons defy the
        Psychology world to say why the
                Hell they take pains
                Not to find inside lanes,
        And at night can't find dip-switches, either.

There's a lassie who's living in Fleet,
Whose neat, very sweet and *petite,*
        But her hair is so red
        That it's frequently led
All traffic to stop in the street.

***

XVIII

BIBLICAL BITS

SAID Adam one morning to Eve:
"I'm finding this hard to believe.
We've raised Cain and Abel,
Who both have a navel,
But the Lord has kept ours up His sleeve."

Said Eve, "All right, things do look grim!
Picking that apple was dim.
But I didn't make
The world's first mistake:
Creation of man's down to HIM!

Lot's sceptical outlook grew rife
As he drew to the end of his life.
Whatever was said,
He would just shake his head
And take with a pinch of his wife.

Joan of Arc, wife of Noah, said, "Let's bring
Every animal under our wing,
Then we can float
In a marvellous boat -
It's the ark erald angels will sing."

David lisped, "Killing Goliath
Wath one of my earnetht dethiath.
Men thought that I couldn't.
They thaid that I wouldn't.
For the thake of thith thtantha, they're liath."

Biblical Bits

A football philosopher, Job,
Was famous all over the glob.
Though short of apparel
And stuck in a barrel,
He thought about Brighton and Hob.

On the road to Damascus, young Saul
Said, "I'm changing my name now, to Paul.
If there's one thing I ain't,
It's a sibilant saint.
Saint Saul sounds appalling, that's all."

The pessimist Job said to Moses,
"A study of life soon discloses
Man has no chance
To make an advance:
One door shuts and another one closes."

Jonah sets out for a sail
That ends in a whale in a gale.
Says Jonah the lonah,
"I don't think I've knonah
Less probable fisherman's tale."

"These tablets of Yours", murmured Moses,
"Are bigger than people suppose. Is
It all right with You
If I take only two
And see what reaction to those is?"

Said Adam, "I don't want to crib
Or complain, but I really do jib
At Creation's great plan,
Making me the one man
With no navel and short of a rib."

Biblical Bits

Exactly like Sodom, Gomorrah
Met its end in fire, brimstone and horrah,
    Absolving the prophet
    They'd told to come ophet
For saying there'd be no tomorrah.

One day, at a wedding in Canaan,
They found there was no wine remanaan.
    A water-based miracle
    Sent the host lyrical,
But possibly took some explanaan.

***

XIX

THE NATIONAL HEALTH

A tradition that surgeons won't break
Involves all the clobber they take,
    Including the masks -
    So that if someone asks,
No-one knows who has made the mistake.

A child psychiatrist's glee
Was boundless the morning that he
    Ensured callers saw
    Pinned up on his door:
"At din-din, weturning at fwee."

The frigate's MO has a few
Ideas of his own which are new.
    When the whole crew felt rummy,
    He looked at each tummy
And called it a navel review.

A dentist, while living in Louth,
Was dismayed that he'd had to move South.
    It's hard to assess
    His extra distress:
His job keeps him down in the mouth.

The National Health

. . . keeps him down in the mouth

The National Health

A reverent-type silence abounds:
On the ward, a consultant expounds.
Pre- and post-surgical,
Almost liturgical:
Hospital Pope on his rounds.

Dieticians lead lives which are planned
On eating which gets out of hand.
They note with a gloat
When we push out the bloat
And they live off the fat of the land.

Embryologists' favourite sport -
Making babies where Nature scores nought -
Means taking their places
In egg-and-sperm races:
Call them God (in the final resort).

Though slimming is never a crime,
It is without reason or rime.
Until it grows bigger,
An hour-glass figure
Will just be a plain waist of time.

A hospital porter in Crewe
Takes his work out on shopping trips, too.
A stiff on his trolley,
Though not very jolly,
Clears the way to the front of the queue.

While taking his FRCS,
Fred sawed the wrong leg off, no less.
Examiners came
And thought it a shame,
But called him a partial success.

The National Health

Fred's arms, legs and back were his chief
Causes of pain, angst and grief.
        Then a kind surgeon said
        Amputating his head
Might produce almost total relief.

        Said the midwife, "Your labour, by rights,
        Ought not to have lasted five nights.
                I can only suggest
                We could hope for the best
        If you stopped and we took off your tights."

A bank robber got a good start
Through a lapse in midwifery's art.
        His mother wore tights
        In labour five nights,
And he was born looking the part.

        A baffled heart patient from Skye
        Awoke from his op with a cry:
                "It's Pacemaker Day!
                Can anyone say
        How on earth I shall manage to die?"

A dapper new surgeon appeared
With a carefully trimmed goatee beard.
        With a well-groomed moustache,
        The effect was *panache,*
But some of us thought she was weird.

        A fed-up psychologist found
        That his thinking was apt to astound,
                But insisted that saps
                In reversed baseball caps
        Needed heads turned the other way round.

The National Health

A dental mechanic in Dover
Made teeth for the pooch he calls Rover,
Who'll begin with a grin
To chew his way in,
And bark when his cusp runneth over.

A surgeon of limited vision
Agreed, "I can't cut with precision.
And I have to concur,
Every op's just a blur -
But the mask always hides indecision."

His stethoscope clamped to his head,
The doctor, stone deaf, sadly said,
"There isn't, I fear,
Much going on here."
"Perhaps", Fred suggested, "I'm dead."

A deaf boffin's failure to follow
Instructions caused laughs that were hollow.
When you're asked to design
A heart drug, that's fine -
But his hearthrug was quite hard to swallow.

The delivery suite was struck dumb
By an ugly new baby in Brum.
Before he could cry,
His face explained why
The midwife was smacking his mum.

***

XX

LAWFUL OCCASIONS

WHEN called to the Bar, Fred said, "Honey,
Don't you think that at times life is funny?
As a child, there were sighs
If they knew I told lies,
But now I can do it for money."

As fine Europeans, we've faced
Absurdities too good to waste.
A nice one from Brussels -
Just flexing its mussels? -
Says snails are now fish (but land-based).

"What's your plea?" cross-eyed judge asked O'Dowd.
"Not guilty, sorr", answered McLeod.
"Shut up, you fool!"
Cried the judge - and O'Toole
Said, "Oi must have been thinking out loud."

Your life expectation was short
If the judge put his cap on in court,
And you ended, by heck,
With a rope round your neck
As your visible means of support.

There are those who think tights are sublime
For hiding their face at a crime.
For one, the appeal
Was largely surreal:
Wife's mum had them on at the time.

Lawful Occasions

A smooth-tongued attorney whose grip
On dealings with clients may slip,
Can then turn and say,
"Go to hell!" in a way
That hints it's a really good trip.

There are few who do not understand
The lore of the law of the land.
The lore says the law
Is an ass. What is more,
The law seems to bray on demand.

We love being kind to the criminal
Whose chance of reforming is minimal.
We're in such a jolly daze,
We send him on holidays:
The pleasure we get is subliminal.

Cried the lawyer outside heaven's gate,
"I'm too young to die! Can't you wait?"
Said St Peter, "Compliance
With time charged to clients
Gives your age as at least 98."

Said His Honour, "The trouble with me
Is the ease with which I seem to see
The truth on each side,
Which the other's denied,
And judge that I have to agree."

An ambitious young barrister, Toya,
Caught stealing a gallery's Goya,
Explained, "It's my aim
To attain greater fame
As a practising criminal lawyer."

XXI
ANIMAL ANTICS

A remarkable beast is the cat.
It repeatedly demonstrates that
When it falls from a tree,
Unlike you and me,
It won't hit the ground and go *Splat!*

I have yet to discover the relevance
Of seven benevolent elevance -
But one pachyderm
Could spend a short term
On reception, to answer the televance.

A dog's a divine indication:
Bark-to-front was the game of Creation -
While it's clear that that
Transmogrified cat
Is probably planned purrmewtation.

A rose-coloured swan? Yes, that's right.
It's not an unusual sight.
What everyone knows is,
The spectrum of roses
Includes quite a lot which are white.

Howdah is short for a bit
Of a challenge to skill and to wit.
If you don't get a bunk
From an elephant's trunk,
Howdahyahknah where to sit?

. . . so the kid made his bid

Animal Antics

Sammy Snail gave his mother a hug
And announced, "It's the old travel bug!
    Suckers itchy as hell!
    Must come out of my shell!"
So the kid made his bid - as a slug.

Said a glow-worm, "I don't feel right.
I've just had a terrible night.
    The problem at essence
    Is my incandescence:
I can't sleep a wink in the light."

A man called today on a camel,
In a suit made of steel and enamel.
    The beast was a brute
    And the suit didn't suit
The lines of so lumpy a mammal.

Cuckoos invade without booking:
Lay eggs when there's nobody looking.
    Once spring has sprung,
    They don't feed their young:
They fight over oo does the cucking.

In the bar, a white horse soon saw red -
Appalled, as a customer said,
    "What a daft thing to do!
    Naming Scotch after you!"
Said the horse, "Neigh! There's nowt wrong wi' Fred."

With foresight and planning, we ought
To make guard-your-garden a sport
    By laying hot bricks
    Where cats do their tricks,
To give messy mogs paws for thought.

Animal Antics

Said the doctor, "I'm sure that the cause
Of your pain is this parrot of yours,
Which you keep on your head."
The parrot then said,
"Can this head be removed from my claws?"

Said a curious elephant, "Spell
It out for me, Mouse: kindly tell
Me why you're so small."
"No problem at all,"
Said the mouse. "I just haven't been well."

For a crab, there is no way of knowing
Where on earth it is to-ing or fro-ing.
With a feeling that's sinking,
And lateral jinking,
It sees where it's passing, not going.

A curious beast is the elephant:
Too large to be really irrelephant.
From all that one sees,
It can uproot small trees
Without even feeling malephalent.

Our tortoise was shy, we could tell;
Withdrawn; introverted as well.
We've done what we could -
Maybe more than we should:
He's now come right out of his shell.

Said Daisy the cow, with a gloat,
"I'm pleased, I admit, when I note
The disease BSE*
Does not affect me:
I'm ever so glad I'm a goat."

* BSE: the so-called "Mad Cow Disease."

Animal Antics

They say fish is good for the brain:
Will somebody kindly explain
    Why are cod, hake or skate
    Which come to my plate
So dim they could safely complain?

A fellow who cuddled a croc
Said, "Though people point and make mock,
    I worship her dearly,
    Sincerely, though clearly,
Her love bites can come as a shock."

Said Fred, "I would like some advice
On shoeing a horse. Though it's nice
    To fashion a shoe,
    What on earth should I do
With a horse that falls out of the vice?"

The camel said, "Allah is wise:
My lashes keep sand from my eyes.
    My hump is for drought,
    When there's no food about. . .
All of which makes my zoo a surprise."

In one of their small-hours debates,
A red-eyed old ewe told her mates,
    "It would make us poor sheep less
    Consistently sleepless,
If people could jump over gates."

Henry the pooch could not quell
His awesomely doggy-breath smell.
    Hal soon became
    His diminutive name,
As it meant halitosis as well.

Animal Antics

The crew of an old submarine
Never knew what excitement there'd been
    As they went on their way
    In the ocean one day:
"Tin of people!" exclaimed a sardine.

A noisome young oyster would hustle
At the very first hint of spring's rustle.
    This flashy crustacean
    Caused quite a sensation:
Played the fool by the pool, pulled a mussel.

There's a parrot called Poll and she begs
That no-one should call her the dregs,
    Although she gets frisky,
    Gulping down whisky,
And then lays a clutch of scotch eggs.

Said a cow to a sheep in the dark,
"Excuse me, but did you just bark?"
    Said the sheep to the cow,
    "It's wonderful how
Linguistics can be such a lark!"

Said a happy young butterfly, "Few
Can suspect - well, I hadn't a clue
    Until I got changed -
    That Nature arranged
This thing for us tadpoles to do."

A thoroughly unimpressed sheep
Said, "I find it's a bind, though I keep
    On jumping this stile,
    That after a while
I lose count and I'm still not asleep."

Animal Antics

With dogs in the dark, when you've got 'em,
Their eyes make it easy to spot 'em.
But, researchers have found,
The other way round,
They're best with two beads up their bottom.

Cows and goats give us milk, but we wonder
At Nature's quite serious blunder.
I have to report
Pigs' legs are so short,
The bucket just won't quite go under.

When pushed by a cuckoo he knew
From his perch in the gardens at Kew,
A pigeon was heard
As he stuttered, "My word!
C-coo! It's a cuckoo *c-coup*!"

Using rain from the heavens above,
And moved by compassion and love,
Is a Frenchman who blethers,
As he bathes a bird's feathers,
"It's *eau* for the wings of a dove."

Uncanny occurrences strike
More often, perhaps, than you'd like -
But you soon get a feel
For the weird and surreal:
I've been told by a fish on a bike.

A fishpond is there to enjoy,
But the pleasure's a thing fish destroy
By hiding - but why?
Can it be that they're shy?
Well, no - though they're certainly koi.

XXII

MARRIAGE LINES

YOU had to admire the groom's graces
In all of the honeymoon places.
In order to hide
His wife's status as bride,
He insisted she carried the cases.

In the bridal suite, evening approached,
And the newly-weds' fears were broached.
"That water bed might
Not be right for the night:
If the place catches fire, we'll be poached!"

Steve - Bill's son by Diane (his first wife) -
Wed Dad's next wife's mother - what strife!
Bill's second wife, Mandy?
Bill's step-grandchild! And he?
Dad-in-law to her mother. That's life!

On his wedding day, Fred made it clear
That he'd be the boss, never fear.
He would have the last word -
And that's what's occurred:
He has the last *three*! "Yes, my dear."

Best man - what a clown! - doesn't bring
A small band of gold. There's a sting:
The day has now got
The thing he has not:
Technical term - hollow ring.

Marriage Lines

The bride's mother anxiously told her,
"You can see how his grievances smoulder.
    He's just like his dad,
    A well-balanced lad -
Because of a chip on each shoulder."

A bride's starry eyes soon grow dim:
They become sort of steely and grim.
    Ambition will falter:
    Hymn, aisle and *altar*
Are turned into *I'll alter him.*

"We thought that your marriage arrangement
Had ended in mutual estrangement.
    We heard you'd been jilted."
    He answered, quite stilted,
That that was a prior engagement.

Fred lurched in the church on demanding
A drink with the 'groom he was landing.
    It was, though, perhaps,
    His collapse in the apse
Which finally fouled up his standing.

In church, the bride's mother said, "Dear,
Your way to success is quite clear.
    He'll lead, but you'll find,
    If you push from behind,
He'll go any way that you steer."

At the weepiest wedding for years,
The bride and her folks sobbed their fears.
    The bridesmaids and guests
    All watered their chests,
And even the cake was in tiers.

Marriage Lines

The royal pair could not agree,
Except on one thing - to be free,
Leaving Charles on his own
In his wait for the Throne:
The King and Di wasn't to be.

Fred's blood, without warning, congealed
On the day his fiancée revealed:
"A society wedding
Is where we are heading."
The Co-op had never appealed.

Wedding day tears aren't a fake -
But though people cry by mistake,
No lachrymose guest,
However distressed,
Is quite as cut up as the cake.

A marriage may lack the ability
To maintain its romance and virility -
But Nature is kind:
In their place, you will find
Incontinence, maybe senility.

Feminists proudly declare
That women wreck marriages*; swear
They equal a man
In spoiling God's plan
And constantly doing their share.

* The General Synod in 1998 approved a new wedding service in which the phrase, *Those whom God hath joined together, let no man put asunder*, was replaced with . . . *let no ONE put asunder.*

***

XXIII

DOMESTIC ISSUES

WASHING UP is a task that's conducive
To dismay in the brash (or reclusive).
On achieving your goal,
You tip out the bowl -
And the tea spoon that's always elusive.

Writes Consumer (Confused), of Shoreditch:
"Electricity bills are a bitch.
Light, Plug and Socket
All make the things rocket -
But they can be settled with Switch."

DIY is a national disaster,
Seeking skills no home-maker can master.
It's his way of proving
(Losing tools without moving)
He needs all those holes in the plaster.

Her swain doesn't often drink hooch.
He owns neither moggy nor pooch.
Her joy is not queered
Because of his beard:
She just takes the rough with the smooch.

The large, rusting tank was *in situ,*
Then it dropped on the sitter - to wit, you.
Yet next day you faced doom
In that same smallest room:
The dare of the bog, sir, that hit you!

Domestic Issues

A sweet-smelling Zurich-based gnome
Likes to freshen himself and his home.
Aerosols set him raving:
Wrong choice after shaving
Can fill up an armpit with foam.

A culinary wiz shows obedience
To cook-books - except that expedience
Induces contortions
With volumes, proportions,
Temperatures, times and ingredience.

Propinquity CAN be a strain
On relations - a relative pain.
You should carefully think
Whom you plan to propink,
And ponder your prospects of gain.

Said Katie, "How do you enhance a
Life with a man who's a dancer?
Flamenco rules Pete.
I must keep him sweet:
Once he's stamping his feet, I've no answer."

Selective weed-killers affect
A lawn, which they feed and protect
By meeting its needs,
While killing the weeds -
Well, the weeds they decide to select.

Toast is a food of renown:
You cannot be sure it will brown,
And yet it is able
To jump off the table
And always land butter side down.

Domestic Issues

"Cementing the lawn", murmured Fred,
Saved cutting the grass, but it's led,
    Whenever it rains,
    To a shortage of drains
And rowing boat trips to the shed."

A happy inventor in Troon
Said his new prongless fork was a boon.
    Soup didn't slip through,
    Which likewise was true
Of porridge: he'd call it a spoon.

Although I am possibly dumb, what
I confess is eluding me somewhat
    Is the charm that lies in
    All those seeds and tough skin
Of that ugly small fruit called the kumquat.

AIDS TO LIVING

There's no real way of concealing
That mixers are very appealing.
    They really are clever:
    Without one, she'd never
Get fruit cakes all over the ceiling.

A VCR's role is to break
What spirit you have as you take
    Long hours on the floor,
    To peer and to pore,
And record lots of things by mistake.

... a snatch of *Blue Moon*

Domestic Issues

It is kind of the cactus-type dahlia
Not to act all unkind and assahlia -
Unlike the quite truculent
Cactus-type succulent,
Which likes using spikes to impahlia.

We love our dish-washing machine.
Such sparkle we never have seen!
But now we wash up
Not a solit'ry cup,
Our elbows are not quite so clean.

A mobile phone will deny
All access to people who buy.
When they've upped and they've gone,
They don't switch it on,
So you ring and don't get a reply.

A chambermaid based at the Hyatt
Has two ways to make the guests riot.
She likes to annoy some
With noise that is noisome,
And others, by keeping quite quiet.

With a humour which possibly leans
To the cruel, though you know what he means,
A man tends to croon
A snatch of *Blue Moon,*
When his wife's bending down, wearing jeans.

Good neighbours bring joy that's immense -
But sometimes, it's hard to commence.
On hearing that Harry has
Broken down barriers,
We learn he was taking a fence.

Domestic Issues

"Tongue is a meat", Susan said,
"From the mouth of some cow that it's fed.
That sounds so unpleasant,
I think for the present
I'll just have a boiled egg instead."

Security lamps are a lark,
Delighted home-owners remark.
They light when you're there,
To give you a scare,
And they help burglars see in the dark.

Cinnamon, mixed in a trice
With currants, milk, water, eggs, spice,
Salt, butter, flour, peel
And yeast, makes a meal
Which is called hot cross bun - and it's nice!

Fred is the lad who demurred
When he saw that a watch is absurd:
Hour hand is cute -
Unlike minute, minute -
With second hand making a third.

Their marriage is needing repair,
So the Smiths find an expert to share
Their problem. Smith cries,
"I'm surprised at the lies!
Whatsername says I don't care!"

They've put tax on gas and inspire
The feeling, as all bills go higher,
That a coal-effect blaze,
As long as it stays,
Means the VAT really is in the fire.

* VAT was added to gas and electricity bills in April 1994.

Domestic Issues

A butler whose tea tray had slipped,
Through not being properly gripped,
Agreed, "That lacked subtlety:
I don't like to bubtlety
When standards are deemed to have dipped."

You've no earthly reason to grin!
Forgetting my birthday's a sin!
I'm going to tell Mother!
Forgot? You're my brother!
My brother? Ye gods, you're my twin!

Mum looked at the turkey, "Oh, heck!
You'll make me a gibbering wreck!
I've trussed you, I've plucked you,
I've stuffed you, I've cooked you. . .
I'm blowed if I'm wringing your neck!"

"With butter and marge", murmured Fred,
"The difference is all in your head -
So I'll remain mellow
As long as it's yellow
And tends to go flat when it's spread."

Said a case-hardened mother from Crewe,
"Potty training's no mystery: you
Can't fail if you try,
As next day they'll be dry.
It's a help if they're twelve when you do."

Two characteristics of paint
Will irritate sinner or saint:
Its reluctance to flow
Where intended to go,
And its splash in a flash where it ain't.

Domestic Issues

Fred fashioned a love nest for two
In a railway carriage at Crewe.
But he puts out his back
With his push up the track,
Whenever his wife's on the loo.

Despair's in the air as she wails,
"I've had to start painting my nails!
I took some advice
On getting them nice,
On finding that wallpaper fails."

Said Dorothy, there in Glengarry,
"My sister should go off and marry.
Through no fault of mine,
She was named Caroline,
And now we get called Dot and Carrie."

Please, why aren't my biscuit tins square?
Not the round ones, which always play fair,
But the "square", which employ
Such an evil *trompe d'oeil,*
That lids don't quite fit. I go spare!

Said a lady whose snoring had led
To sharpish exchanges in bed,
"I do all that I can
To delight the old man,
And that's why I sleep in the shed."

Their friends are all deeply upset,
With a sadness they'll never forget.
Jack and Jill, it appears,
Were happy for years -
Then fate took a hand, and they met.

Domestic Issues

It's known as a mobile phone,
But if it's not carried or thrown,
　　It is roughly as able
　　As our kitchen table
To go anywhere on its own.

　　Eating's a joy you can't beat.
　　I eat and I eat and I eat.
　　　　I taste it and swallow,
　　　　Put more in to follow,
　　And curse when I find I'm replete.

Their coffee was always the source
Of marital angst - and of course,
　　When he drained the last pot,
　　He knew that he'd got
What looked to be grounds for divorce.

　　Said Susie, "I smoke: you can tell,
　　From the fact that I cough rather well,
　　　　And my fingers are stained
　　　　And I'm plainly lame-brained,
　　And I have such a terrible smell."

Sunset View: when we saw it, we knew it
Was the house we should buy. *Let us do it!*
　　But the middle *N-S*
　　Has been stolen. I guess
That all we're now viewing is suet.

　　Fifi, who's living in Nantes,
　　Would love to assist her old antes,
　　　　Whose home's Aix-les-Bains -
　　　　So there's no way she cains,
　　'cos Fifi's in Nantes and she cantes.

XXIV

A LITTLE LEARNING

WITH space being probed, it is worth
A prayer that we'll yet see the birth
Of efforts confined
To trying to find
Intelligent life here on earth.

A limbless explorer once said,
"If you're lost, eat yourself, or you're dead.
Experience shows
You should start with your toes
And work your way up to your head."

That lovely old city of Rheims
Is clearly not quite what it seems.
It doesn't make sense,
But the French call it Rense.
Their English is worse than one dreams.

A studious fellow called Ray
Read Roget's *Thesaurus* each day.
If you said, "How are you?"
He'd reply, "Ticky-boo,
Fine, thriving, well, super, OK."

Mixed infants, when drawing their God,
Produce a peculiar bod:
A stick-limbed Almighty,
Triangular nightie,
Small head and huge navel - quite odd.

A Little Learning

Education gurus' Holy Grail
Is a system where kids cannot fail.
    They set them exams
    Babes could do in their prams.
(Pocket aids do the sums they entail).*

* A situation which the Government decided to rectify in 1998.

Where learning makes barely a ripple,
The result is a lit'rary cripple.
    Asked, "Do you like Kipling?"
    A slip of a stripling
Said, "Nobody's taught me to kiple."

Formulae normally faze
The people whose maths are a maze.
    The rhomboid or spherical,
    Pure or numerical,
Lays a haze on their gaze lasting days.

The selection committee was there.
The dragon declared, "I'm the chair."
    The potential professor
    Was quick to assess her,
But sat on her, just for a dare.

Even numbers, it's said, up from two,
Are sums of two prime numbers*. Who
    First thought this one out
    Is open to doubt -
But no-one has proved it's not true.

* A prime number is one which will not make a whole number when divided, except when divided either by itself or 1.

A Little Learning

A bomb-making expert from Herne
Was blown up, which caused some concern.
With not enough boffin
To fill up a coffin,
The funeral was pray-as-you-urn.

A scientist based in Belize
Said, "I work pretty much as I please.
My research is so pure,
I have now found a cure
For which there is no known disease."

Computers fall prey to the ranks
Of hackers whose light-fingered pranks
Let them take large amounts
From people's accounts.
They work as a gang called The Banks.

The *fugit* that happens to *tempus* is
Approved by professors with emphasis.
Their working life's span
Brings emeritus man
Instead of *(Retd)* (in parenthesis).

Behavioural scientists say
The things that we do every day
Can give them a clue
To our inner selves, too
(If they're not barking up the wrong *trait*).

Said a watt to an ohm, "I don't know
How you make me completely aglow.
Why on earth is my light
So abundantly bright?"
Said the ohm, "My resistance is low."

A Little Learning

Since *twos* (rhymed with *choose*) proves to be
A singular (odd) plural, we
Must ask if you knew
Two is singular, too.
(Its plural is *twos*). QED.

Discovery's pace, which was fair,
Caused the flat-earth brigade to declare
That they'd got it all wrong.
(And it may not be long
'til Fred gives up thinking it's square).

Have you heard what's occurred with the surd,
That icon whose purpose was blurred?
Inscrutable core
Of algebra law:
Where's it gone? What's it done? Not a word!

An explorer, safe home in Nuneaton,
Insisted, "State schools can't be beaten.
When cannibals came,
It seemed such a shame
That all my companions were Eton."

A student of English at Hook
Gave syntax and semtex a look -
But being a dunce,
Confused them at once
And blew up his exercise book.

We could see, quite indelibly pasted
On his face, the success he had tasted.
"Whom are you?" he would sneer,
In a tone that made clear
His night-school class hadn't been wasted.

XXV

MERELY MALES

SAID a weak-willed old fellow named Dewar,
Whose actions grew slower and fewer:
"I was once, you could tell,
As uncertain as hell -
But now I just cannot be sure."

A man with four legs and a beak
Said, "Kindly don't call me unique.
It's a much-abused word.
I have always preferred
To be thought of as simply a freak."

A factor that merits applause is
His labour for all kinds of causes.
He has unflagging zest
Then a bit of a rest:
That zest never wanes but it pauses.

The greeting was heated, not warm,
Which was nothing much out of the norm:
"You're gormless!" said he.
I replied, "I agree:
I've not got a sign of a gorm."

"You uncouth, gormless nincompoop!" storms
A critic, requesting reforms.
I reply with a whoop:
"I am couth and compoop!
What's more, I am brimming with gorms."

Merely Males

A man for whom everything shows
Back-to-front, murmured, “That’s how it goes.
        It ensures what I see
        Is peculiar to me:
That’s as plain as the face on your nose.”

        Being jabbed with a pin will convert
        A sleeper who’s prone and inert
                Into conduct extremely
                Uncouth and unseemly.
        He’ll revert, somewhat curt, to the ert.

A petty crook slipped, in a daze,
Into new-laid foundations in Hayes.
        As a chance, it was minimal:
        This now-hardened criminal
Has found that he’s set in his ways.

GOING FOR IT BALD-HEADED

When baldness begins, it’s not rare
For horrified man to prepare
        For meeting his dome
        In secret at home,
With a wig: it’s a breadth of fresh hair.

When baldness begins, what is more,
And a wig’s on the point that is sore,
        It’s because man expects
        To hide his defects.
That’s what a flaw-covering’s for.

Merely Males

Despite the beliefs we've been bred on,
In spite of the tenets we tread on,
It's clear that we can
See the chief end of man
Is the end we can see with the head on.

The ageing of man is what shows
With a scalp that quite suddenly glows.
What grew on the head
Grows backwards instead,
Emerging in tufts from his nose.

A frantic young fellow from Skye
Burst in on his doctor to cry,
With a fearful finality,
"I'm a split personality!
And what makes it worse, so am I!"

A hard-working jogger from Skye
Ran 10 miles a day, wet or dry.
When asked to explain,
He replied in great pain,
"I want to be fit when I die."

Said a miserable fellow from Cork,
"I always drink soup with a fork.
While it drips through the spaces,
I watch people's faces:
They're all too embarrassed to talk."

A sociable Scot in Siam
Said, "I'm not at all sure who I am.
If I am who I think,
You can buy me a drink.
If I'm not. . . I shall still have a dram."

Merely Males

Said a word-blind young man from Lee Bank,
"Karate's a butch way to swank."
Alas, the poor bloke, he
Next found karaoke,
And sang with great verve to a plank.

A wealthy old buffer in Mayfair
Was wishing that Nature would play fair.
"There's pleasure to take,
Sinking teeth in a steak -
But now, when I sink them, they stay there."

A cow-poke confessed to his pards,
"I guess I'm concerned as regards
My shortness of breath.
Shucks! Worried to death!
It shouldn't occur, playing cards."

A very old fellow in Ryde
Had a theory on why he'd not died.
He was asked what accounted
For how the years mounted.
"Just breathing, I think", he replied.

A fellow with minimal brain
Cried, "Bother! I've done it again!
It's the fourth time I've come
From Glasgow to Brum,
Forgetting to get on the train."

A fellow with failed self-delusion
Proclaimed, "I'm the best!" - an allusion
Which people perceived
He never believed
And caused him no little confusion.

Merely Males

Said an anxious young man from St Just,
"I won't take my nostrils on trust.
Nose hair, so I'm told,
Will appear when I'm old:
But meanwhile, what keeps out the dust?"

A very bald gentleman said,
"Although I'm impeccably bred,
I am jealous and swear
At a full head of hair,
As I have a full head of head."

A sunny young man at Loch Ness,
Whom hardly a thing could depress,
Said one cause for fretting
Was very upsetting:
His failure to suffer from stress.

Alopecia, of course, is not rare:
It's stress that's believed to be there -
Though Fred couldn't find
He'd a thing on his mind,
Apart from the loss of his hair.

"Please, doctor", Fred said, "I'm perplexed.
A man who's less mild would be vexed -
But I think, though it's risible,
That I'm mute and invisible,
So I wonder. . ." The doctor said, *"Next!"*

A forgetful old fellow from Fakenham
Had memory pills and kept shakenham -
A rattling good ploy
Which he seemed to enjoy,
But forgot he was meant to be takenham.

Merely Males

A beau who for years had been hunted
By girls, found his charms had been blunted
By food he'd encased,
Which had all gone to waist
And finally made him beau-fronted.

An expert in polished titanium
Had a sharply concave sort of cranium,
Into which he would slip,
Once he'd burnished the dip,
A rather attractive geranium.

Fear of fashion consistently keeps
The diarist so fraught that he weeps:
"I dare not be dressed
Like Brummel or Geste,
In case I get known as Beau Pepys."

Said a man with a band on his head,
"Apart from the noise, which I dread,
The brass section's starting
To ruin my parting,
And the flutes are a nuisance in bed."

"I'm dismayed!" Fred exclaimed to his mother.
"I've turned out the same as my brother!
I'm a total calamity -
A split personality,
And each as disliked as the other."

A health food fanatic called Gus
Did a work-out each day without fuss,
But his fitncss rcgimc
Rather ran out of steam
The day he stepped under a bus.

Merely Males

It was terribly easy to sneer
At a man with two mouths and one ear.
From the time he was young
And spoke with forked tongue,
We were rude and he'd only half-hear.

As it's known that the mind has a flaw
Which gives things a seeming *encore,*
With his heart on his sleeve,
Fred will not believe
That he's had *déjà vu* once before.

His travels in various areas
Were frequently very nefarious.
He gleefully went
With evil intent,
And now he is fairly malarious.

An honest young man named Josiah
Said, "People should try to acquire
The instinct to doubt
Any tale I put out.
Believe me, I'm such a damn' liar."

Male torsos grow older and vary:
Thomas Richard, aged two, should be wary.
Hirsute's not cute:
Grown up, he'll transmute
To just being Tom Dick and hairy.

There's a time when a man must decide
On the hair loss he knows he can't hide:
To embrace - if not hug -
A flaw-covering rug,
Or to show how a head's worn with pride.

. . . a flaw-covering rug

Merely Males

A diffident cowboy called Frame
Was quite well prepared when he came:
    His assertiveness course
    Found him there with his horse,
False beard, false moustache and false name.

A man with a face like a ferret
Likes to think that he gets jobs on merit,
    So he's hard to console
    When he's pushed down a hole
For a rabbit: he says he can't bear it.

XXVI

SHALL WE JOIN THE LADIES?

A fanciful woman called Eva
Was known to shun truth like a fever.
When she said to Josiah,
"I am just a born liar",
He flatly refused to believe her.

A female whose figure gets bigure
Will find that it acts as a trigure -
A spur which leaves women
Bromen with slomen
Intent but no practical vigure.

Said a distant relation of mine,
"My beard was always a swine -
And trimmed to the stubble,
It still gives me trouble."
The rest of us think she looks fine.

Fashion's fads? Women ought to resist 'em!
Far better all round if they missed 'em!
Inordinate thighs
With hemlines that rise
Should never be part of the system.

Each person needs someone to treasure;
To share in life's hopes, pain and pleasure.
Though Sue's on the shelf,
She's in love with herself,
And the feeling's returned in full measure.

Shall We Join the Ladies?

A scrawny young lady from Jarrow,
Who squeaked in a range that was narrow,
Was heard to remark,
"As I've legs like a lark,
It's a shame that I sing like a sparrow."

A puzzled young lass called Louise
Has acquired an intriguing disease.
It's not that it's serious -
Just a touch deleterious:
All her parts that were pairs come in threes.

Two bow-legged women intent
On a knock-kneed young fellow from Kent,
Walked one on each side
In formation which cried,
OXO wherever they went.

The prostate's the family bane:
It crops up again and again.
It's caused tribulations
For six generations -
But so far, it's missed Great Aunt Jane.

With women, we always expect 'em
To cope with the ills that affect 'em.
If things aren't as should be
When they've tried D and C,
The next step's hysterical rectum.

Dear Jane, it is plain, has been blest
With a body all men like the best -
With muscular thighs
And biceps that size,
And curly black hairs on her chest.

XXVII

THE MEDIA

A newsreader said, "I deplore
Scottish football results more and more.
I can say *Hamilton*
Academicals 1,
But I fear *Forfar 5 East Fife 4.*"

A wise leader writer's inclined
To see that his job's redefined,
So that readers receive
Only what they believe:
He still leads, but he leads from behind.

The commentary team haven't stopped:
A football is banged, bundled, topped.
But no, it's not kicked:
Other options they've picked
Are lobbed, lifted, poked, prodded, popped.

I've Arrived and can show you the proof:
It's naffin but Gawd's honest troof.
I open me marf
And say fings like *sarf*,
And present telly programmes for yoof.*

* Purveyors of "Estuary English", especially presenters on children's television, have come under fire for their use of the language.

A literate hack is quite rare:
Don't Know hand-in-hand with Don't Care.
A *whom* and a *who*,
Compare with, compare to,
Interchanged with no thought but great flair.

A resourceful reporter called Rose
Was asked by her boss to disclose
What she meant - "GOK" -
On expenses each day.
She shrugged and said, "God only knows."

AS IT HAPPENS

Soccer pundits have surely rehearsed
League tables to bring out their worst
And make our jaws drop:
When a team's "second top",
We guess that they mean second first.

With hurdle race broadcasts, prepare -
Then count the last hurdles in there.
Commentators talk fast. . .
"Third last*, second last*. . ."
But first last's remarkably rare.

* Oddly illogical terminology coined by out-of-breath broadcasters, presumably in the cause of saving syllables.

Though radio tries hard to please,
Its listeners seem ill at ease
If they fail to get talkers -
Just high-wire walkers,
Jugglers, mime and striptease.

Said a journalist, down in Torquay,
"A freelance is what I won't be.
Although it sounds rash,
I do things for cash:
A moneylance doesn't come free."

From the girls in commercials we've seen
For staying unlined and serene,
We now have the notion
We don't need a potion -
Just a face that's no more than sixteen.

FANNY'S FAREWELL

So Fanny* has gone for her harp.
Hope she sits on a corner that's sharp.
Or maybe she's bitchin'
At the stove in Hell's kitchen.
(Her favourite food was the carp).

Oh, Fanny, a happy release
(For those whom you now predecease) -
But carry on carping,
As heavenly harping
Means we down below rest in peace.

* Fanny Cradock, a cantankerous cook who made a 1960s television reputation built entirely on aggressive rudeness. One of her achievements was to appear with a woman who had won a cookery competition - and savage her. She died in 1994, aged 84.

A radio roads commentator
Attributes delays - how I hate her! -
To "an earlier accident",
In case we assume she meant
They're all down to one that came later.

Ahead of's becoming a bore,
But it's used on the air more and more.
It's always said quickly
And ever so slickly
By those who can't manage *before.*

XXVIII

THERE WAS A. . .

There was a's *the limerick mould*
These pages have left in the cold,
So here is a sprinkling
To give just an inkling
Of custom it's time to uphold.

*

THERE was a young lady from Spain,
Who said, "I've a tap and a drain.
Good though these are
For washing the car,
Not having a hose, I refrain."

There was a young fellow called Chas
Who rhymed with his big brother, Jas.
While living in Mdx,
They suffered from hdx,
And that's why they moved out to Mass.

There was a young lady called Cindy,
Who looked at her bridegroom and grinned: "He
May not think it's funny -
But I'm bride and sunny,
While he has become wed and windy."

There was a...

There was a young woman from Crewe,
Who knew Kew would equally do
For a lad writing verse
With a wish to rehearse
A rhyme scheme involving the loo.

There was a young barrister who
Was sometimes a thespian, too.
She forgot torts and fiefs
And abandoned her briefs
For a part in a farce in West Looe.

There was a young curate who raved,
"The pathway to Hades is paved
With well-meant intentions,
But I've no pretensions:
I've never meant well, so I'm saved."

There was a young girl in the Gower,
Who always stayed dressed in the shower.
Her clothes were kept clean
With no washing machine,
But rarely dried out in the hour.

There was a young builder named Gary
Who said, "I've decided to marry.
It's not for her looks
Or the way that she cooks,
It's how many bricks she can carry."

There was a young man from Nastend,
Who could send any friend round the bend.
They never knew why,
When up on a high,
He'd find brand new depths and descend.

There was a...

. . . a primate's the head of the Church

There was a...

There was a young man in Versaille,
Who sailled, "Aille've been swailleped in the aille."
    Jaded but jocular,
    Socked in the ocular,
Trailled to denaille that he'd craille.

    There was an old man in a tree,
    Who called from the top, "Eighty-three
        Years ago, like a mutt,
        I sat on a nut -
    And Mum said to get home for tea."

There was a young lady from Speke,
Whose clothes were high fashion and chic.
    When she fell in a midden
    A farmer had hidden,
Her friends kept away for a week.

    There was a young man from Llanfair
    PG (and the rest - you know where!),
        Who never addressed
        Letters home, as he guessed
    By the time he'd done that, he'd be there.

There was a young lass from Kinsale,
With a nose like a chimpanzee's tail.
    Prehensile proboscis
    Produced a dead-loss kiss
And choked osculatory male.

    There was a young ape whose research
    Made him say, "There's no cause to besmirch
        Little monkeys like me,
        When the whole world can see
    A primate's the head of the Church."

There was a...

There was a young lady from Norwich
Who said, "There's no cause, to my knowledge,
        Why its spelling won't match
        With one of the batch,
College, porridge, acknowledge or *forage.*"

There was a young lady called Liz
Who complained, "I have lost all my fizz.
        I suffer a lot
        With *je ne sais quoi,*
But I don't really know what it is."

There was a young lady named Lottie,
Not bright and undoubtedly dotty,
        Whose bimbo demeanour
        Explained why we'd seen her
Insistently talked of as tottie.

There was a young lady named Hannah,
Who thrust down her throat a large spanner.
        She rejoiced in a voice
        That was noisome by choice,
With no plan for a man in her manner.

There was an old fellow from Quatt,
Who complained of the pains he had got.
        "But I'm long in the tooth,
        And to tell you the truth,
The alternative isn't too hot."

XXIX

MY PIG

MY pig is a beast I admire.
My pig doesn't smell of the byre.
My pig will awaken
Just smelling of bacon,
From pig-naps in front of the fire.

My pig is a glorious beast.
My pig's charms have immensely increased.
If I'm needing my chair,
And my pig's sitting there,
My pig doesn't mind in the least.

My pig and I go for a walk.
My pig's not much given to talk.
My pig soon gets tired.
I know what's required:
A piggy-back brings home the pork.

My pig said, "I hope you don't mind,
But your chatter is such that I find,
Once you've launched into talk
Of sausage and pork,
It starts to get under my rind."

My pig loves his food - he's a nut. He
Gets everything down, soft as putty.
My pig goes and snuffles
In search of his truffles,
But simply won't try a pork butty.

My Pig

. . . pig in the middle

My Pig

My pig said, "These feet I have got,
To take me around, spot to spot,
Are always called trotters,
Although they are not, as
They're likely to lumber, not trot."

My pig said, "I'm feeling quite bitter.
I give up! I'll just be a quitter!
While I've tried since Friday
To keep Britain tidy,
The wife goes on dropping her litter."

My pig just recoiled in confusion,
On hearing my careless allusion
That sketching fried bacon
Implied he had taken
To drawing a pig-like conclusion.

My pig, who quite likes to decide
The family dietary guide,
Yelled - typically nutty -
"How's this for a butty?"
With a slice of brown bread either side.

My pig thought he'd sail on the sea.
My pig bought a dinghy for me.
My pig went afloat
In a pigmy-sized boat.
My pig was pig-sick as can be.

My pig is as fit as a fiddle.
My pig will sing, *Hey, diddle-diddle!*
My pig came to bed
With his pig-wife, which led
Me to feel I was pig in the middle.

My Pig

My pig is a pig of resource.
The ministry's pleased to endorse,
    Now he's just passed his test,
    That he drives with the best -
Which makes him a road hog, of course.

My pig is a pig you can hail.
There aren't many points where he'll fail -
    Though when he plays poker,
    This happy young joker
Can never help wagging his tail.

My pig told his grandmother, "Nan,
Stay awake, please, as long as you can.
    Let's make no mistake,
    You're far nicer awake:
When you're sleeping, you snore like a man."

My pig does not usually cry.
When he did, I went out to see why.
    "You don't give a damn",
    Sobbed my pig. "Here I am,
With a stye in my eye in my sty."

My pig has shown helpful complicity
In sharing his strange eccentricity.
    Every night, for an hour,
    He gives out pig power,
Providing off-pig electricity.

My pig was as chuffed as could be.
"That chap over there", chortled he,
    "With the ring through his nose:
    Do you really suppose
He thinks he's as handsome as me?"

My Pig

My pig is a gullible guy:
He believes what you tell him, that's why.
    He jumped off the roof
    To offer the proof,
When he heard someone say pigs might fly.

My pig gets himself in a state.
My pig hates the workings of fate.
    My pig hates the snuffles
    He needs to get truffles:
He'd like them just served on a plate.

***

XXX

CORRESPONDENCE COURSE

DEAR FATHER, I've gone on the run.
Been having the booze, girls and fun.
But now I've no cash
And I can't cut a dash.
Please send some instanter - Your Son.

Dear Son, Have you ever been had?
Too much, far too soon, and too bad.
Try getting a job,
You consummate slob!
Mum sends best wishes - Your Dad.

Dear Mr Burlington-Burke,
Sorry I've not been at work.
My mother's just died,
My daughter's a bride,
And my wife has run off with some jerk.

Dear Jones, What a terrible tome!
I notice you're writing from Rome.
What plight will you peg
To the Cup's second leg,
When Rovers are playing at home?

Correspondence Course

Dear Sergeant, This charge will abort.
My car simply couldn't cavort
        At eighty, on ice,
        Uphill: please be nice!
Yours faithfully, Asterix Short.

Memo re speeder A Short.
Have read the official report.
        Tell him from me,
        He's out of his tree -
Get stuffed and we'll see him in court.

Dear Pardn'r, That critter looked bleak.
No-one could get him to speak.
        He seemed real blue:
        Was it something to do
With the fact that we lynched him last week?

Dear Pardn'r, I thought that you'd spot him.
I guess he was wishing we'd shot him.
        But he paid for his crimes:
        Though the rope broke ten times,
In the end, like we told him, we got him.

Dear Santa, You might like to hear
What happened at Christmas last year.
        I heard my dad swear
        When he fell up a stair.
Served him right: he was wearing your gear.

Dear Tommy, What sharp little eyes!
That must have been quite a surprise!
        No wonder I found,
        On coming around,
No sign of those awful mince pies.

Correspondence Course

A Basildon beauty grew fond
Of a pen-pal from over The Pond.
    She's checking the ethics
    Of writing from Essex
And forming a Basildon bond.

    Two pen-pals deny that they'll wed:
    Romance won't advance, though not dead.
        While times are inflationary,
        They'll just stand by stationery:
    A stamp costs much less than a bed.

***

XXXI
OCCUPATIONAL HAZARDS

ISTANBUL'S crooked cobbler is prosperous,
With daughters who fizzle like phosphorous.
For young men in fezzes,
The fate of affairs is
Bespoke concrete boots in the Bosporus.

The guru, 92, said, "How sweet!
A birthday cake, laid at my feet!"
He put on his sandals
To blow out the candles,
But couldn't get near for the heat.

MPs never know where they're landing,
Once public opinion is banding
Against them in scandal
Which they cannot handle.
They may lose their seats and their standing.

Genealogists seem to agree
They don't have much reason for glee:
If family history
Remains just a mystery,
It means they've barked up the wrong tree.

It's clever, how traders design
The formulae which will enshrine
The rule which says that
Any price, any VAT,
Must combine to produce 99.

Occupational Hazards

. . . between me and the tree

Occupational Hazards

The tree-cutter said, "I can see,
With hindsight, I have to agree
It's a shame that somehow
I sat on a bough
With the saw between me and the tree."

The draper's assistant looked hurt.
On his first day at work, he was curt.
He said to his boss,
"I'm alas, at a loss:
I simply can't say *short-sleeved shirt.*"

When builders are building a wall
Of bungalow, manor or hall,
You should see what they stick
Behind all that brick:
Posterity's in for a ball.

A plumber in Houston, from Dorset,
Found a pipe that was stuck, and of course it
Inspired him to ask,
As he fell to the task,
"Should I tap it or yank it and faucet?"

A friendly young dancer called Kate
Believes introductions can't wait.
She's making her number
While doing the rumba:
36-24-38.

The sheriff had never rehearsed
Encountering baddies, but nursed
Among his suggestions,
Shoot and ask questions -
Uncertain which process came first.

. . . a very large sticky round head

Occupational Hazards

Kamikaze's for those who like flying,
With particular interest in dying.
Tokyo Joe
Did ten missions. We know
He got this success without trying.

The lollipop lady once said
It could be her diet which led
To her looking so droll,
With a shape like a pole
And a very large sticky round head.

For air stewardesses, the trick
Lies in knowing the job's smart and slick;
Insisting they're thrilled
That they could end up killed,
Saying thanks for a bag full of sick.

The Monarch declared, "I have gone
Off birthdays and suchlike - for none
Of those whom I know
Can make a good show
And sing *Happy birthday to One.*"

Cried a treasure trove hunter, dismayed,
"It hasn't worked out, I'm afraid.
I didn't expect a
New metal detector
Would just keep on finding my spade."

Said a bellringer, ringing in Cheam,
"I find that I run out of steam
If I cling to the rope
In diminishing hope
And wallop my head on the beam."

. . . a way of her own

Occupational Hazards

Cried a gravedigger, seized with self-doubt,
"This can't be what life is about!
I'm new to my role
And I've dug my first hole,
But no-one said how to get out."

There's a lady who is, without doubt,
The best fortune-teller about,
Though she firmly believes
In reading the leaves
In a way of her own - through the spout.

A burglar maintained his mystique
On breaking his wrist while in Leek.
He intoned with a groan
On his hospital phone,
"They're casing the joint, so to speak."

A cabby who lived in Torbay
Rode in style round the streets every day.
But his friends have been told
The taxi's now sold:
The fares outgrew what he could pay.

Though a funeral director's astute,
He knows that he cannot refute,
For all his sobriety
And pomp and propriety,
That burial's an ageist pursuit.

A young lighthouse keeper from Ealing
Met an end that was hardly appealing.
To a crisis he raced
Up the stairs in such haste,
He screwed himself into the ceiling.

Occupational Hazards

When unions unite for a tussle,
There's a fuss and a hustle and bustle,
    A flurry of worry
    And hurry and scurry,
And a flush of industrial muscle.

    Regardless of age, race or sex,
    A common incompetence wrecks
        Potential pig-roasters'
        Publicity posters,
    Which say they're arranging barbeques.

All high-wire walkers ignore
Their personal safety and score
    Resounding success -
    Or else make a mess
When they fall 50ft to the floor.

    A builder gave glib explanations
    Of why he cemented relations:
        "That's not a disaster -
        That's Auntie in plaster.
    Our bond now has concrete foundations."

A boffin took pains to explore
The reason his finger was sore.
    He eyed it and tried it,
    He dyed it and fried it,
And found it was stuck in the door.

    A group of invisible menders
    Have given up bucking the trend, as,
        When they meet, they can't swear
        That there's anyone there.
    They no longer send out agendas.

Occupational Hazards

A lavatory cleaner named Nell
Didn't start her new job very well.
With her very first flush,
Hanging on to her brush,
She swept through the sewer as well.

A peat-cutter's work was a slog,
With visitors always agog
On finding he pandered
To questions on standard
By saying, "Well, basically, bog."

A baffled pathologist said,
"I simply can't think what has led
Some folk to allude
To my being quite rude -
But they say that I cut people dead."

***

XXXII

THE DEMON DRINK

A willing young man in Redhill
Has a job in a bar, but no skill.
The customers grin
At their tankards of gin,
But their beer comes in sixths of a gill.

The landlord who rules at the Star
Has decor that gives you a jar,
Including two nooses
Whose primary use is
When customers hang round the bar.

The locals unite to complain
Of the pub that they won't use again.
They tell you together,
The beer's like the weather:
It's cloudy and looking like rain.

Gushed a lush in a seaside resort,
Drinking gin every night by the quart:
"No mixers for me!
I'm sure you can shee
It'sh the gin that'sh the tonic, old shport!"

A don who was one of Emmanuel's
Thought he heard someone say, "Try Jack Daniels."
'twas a dog-breeder's cry
Which set him awry:
The lady had asked, "Why lack spaniels?"

The Demon Drink

Said Michael, who came from Tralee,
"Oi drink too much beer when at sea.
    When Oi'm in me bunk,
    As drunk as a skunk,
They shout that it's rissoles for tea."

Said an upright young lady named Win,
"Gin is the pathway to sin.
    If it's not too much trouble,
    I'll start with a double:
That could be the way to begin."

The night that Fred really got canned
Was when he was out with the band.
    He went home in style
    For nearly a mile,
Then somebody stepped on his hand.

A lady quite truly devout
Once shocked all her friends round about.
    She explained, "Very few
    Have a clue what I'll do
On a gin and a bottle of stout."

A drink where you're needing some *nous* is
The one that they call Mickey Mouse*: is
    It clear what you do
    When ordering two?
Mickey Mice, or else two Mickey Mouses?

* A Mickey Mouse is a lager-and-bitter.

Said Maisie, "The beauty of sin,
No matter what age you begin,
    Is the way that it seems
    To improve on your dreams,
Once you start with a very small gin."

The Demon Drink

A drunk, nearly out on his feet,
Staggered in with a bright parakeet.
        Cried the barman, old Pat,
        "Where DID you get that?"
And the bird said, "They litter the street."

Said a lad whom good grace had deserted,
Of a lady with whom he had flirted,
        "The way I drink Smirnoff
        Has not been a turn-off.
In fact, she has been quite diverted."

***

XXXIII

A CHANCE OF A GHOST

SAID a vicar, invited to look
At spirits at Newnham, near Hook:
"Do we begin
On your bottle of gin,
Or open my exorcise book?"

Anne Boleyn's ghost said, "No fun
Is involved in the old ramparts run.
My head has no charm,
Tucked under my arm:
I tell you, the thing weighs a ton."

There are those who think walking through walls
Must be fun - but the fact is, it palls.
I know one old shade
Who is always dismayed
And has had one or two nasty falls.

A ghost who was whiter than white
Said, "I've been in the graveyard tonight.
I met some young people
Beneath the church steeple:
I tell you, they gave me a fright."

A ghost who was new said, "I'm bored!
I've died: where on earth's the reward?
He's now designated
As poltergeist-rated,
And throws things while others applaud.

A Chance of a Ghost

The ghost of Bill Sikes was agog,
On meeting the vicar in fog.
    The vicar said, "Bill,
    Your involvement is nil:
I'm just exorcising your dog."

    The haunting of rural retreats,
    Like castles and old country seats,
        Quite suddenly ceased -
        Not due to a priest,
    But simply a shortage of sheets.

Two golfers had just had a jar.
One said, as they walked to the car,
    "I suppose, at the most,
    That a poorly old ghost
Would be known as a shade under par."

    A ghost in the Eagle and Star
    Ordered gin and was given a jar -
        Not of gin, but a shock:
        The landlord said, "Cock,
    Spirits aren't served in this bar."

Though the poltergeist said he was sure
We'd find him both helpful and pure,
    We can't think what on earth
    His presence is worth:
He still throws. No-one knows what's the cure.

***

XXXIV
A CONCENTRATED SPELL

To try to be different, rejoice and submit
A change to the limerick ideal: your verse
Has rhymes letter-based and rejuvenated.
An oddly juvenile avenue of the Limerick:
Just a spell of my idiocy. I hope you like it.

THE MESSAGE CAN ADJUST: IT'S A MAD LIMERICK. . .

T-O/-T-R-Y/-T-O-B
E-D/-I-F-F/-E-R-E
N-T/-R-E-J
O-I/-C-E-A
N-D/-S-U-B/-M-I-T

A-C/-H-A-N/-G-E-T
O-T/-H-E-L/-I-M-E
R-I/-C-K-I
D-E/-A-L-Y
O-U/-R-V-E/-R-S-E

H-A/-S-R-H/-Y-M-E
S-L/-E-T-T/-E-R-B
A-S/-E-D-A
N-D/-R-E-J
U-V/-E-N-A/-T-E-D.

A-N/-O-D-D/-L-Y-J. . .

A Concentrated Spell

A-N/-O-D-D/-L-Y-J
U-V/-E-N-I/-L-E-A
V-E/-N-U-E
O-F/-T-H-E
L-I/-M-E-R/-I-C-K

J-U/-S-T-A/-S-P-E
L-L/-O-F-M/-Y-I-D
I-O/-C-Y-I
H-O/-P-E-Y
O-U/-L-I-K/-E-I-T.

T-H/-E-M-E/-S-S-A
G-E/-C-A-N/-A-D-J
U-S/-T-I-T
S-A/-M-A-D
L-I/-M-E-R/-I-C-K.

***

XXXV

A LENGTHY BUSINESS

A man with a very long face
Explained that he felt out of place.
He said, "I have found,
With my chin on the ground,
I fill up all vertical space."

A man with a very long foot
Found uses to which he could put
That enormous supporter,
Like walking on water,
And scraping tall flues free of soot.

A man with a very long name
Said, "I think it's a bit of a shame:
It goes on for ages
And takes several pages,
And Dad's is exactly the same."

A man with a very long neck
Said, "I'm not very happy, by heck!
There's been a suggestion
That meal to digestion
Is taking three weeks: I'm a wreck!"

A man with a very long nose
Displays all its uses at shows:
Spreading the mustard
And stirring the custard
And hanging up newly-washed poes.

A Lengthy Business

A man with a very long pause
Between breaths is a serious cause
        Of concern to his wife,
        Who fears for his life
As she waits for an hour between snores.

        A man with a very long way
        To go to the station each day
                Strides on in silence
                For mile after mile an' s-
        imply has nothing to say.

XXXVI

HOLIDAY TIME

WAY out on Windermere, clowning,
Ignoring her friends, who were frowning,
Dawn took her small daughter
A walk on the water.
Death from asphyxia by drowning.

Proud Pisans quite rightly insisted
That nothing else like it existed.
Inside an hour
Of building their tower,
They said that it ought to be listed.

The British abroad have no doubt
What *entente cordiale* is about.
The natives' daft lingo
Does not make your grin go:
You just wave your arms while you shout.

A holidaymaker from Clee
Has just spent a week by the sea.
The weather was nice:
It rained only twice -
For four days and later for three.

The French, as a race, cannot see
Why the rest of the world should agree
That the one thing they aren't
Is full of *entente,*
Savoir faire, joie de vivre and *esprit.*

Holiday Time

. . . my first step in China

Holiday Time

A holidaymaker called Vera
Met a friend on a trip to Madeira.
    Said the friend, "Nay, it's queer,
    Us meeting out 'ere."
Vera said, "And I've walked, which is queerer."

    A fearless explorer once said,
    "I'll never get out of my head
        My first step in China -
        In nightshirt (designer) -
    One day as I climbed out of bed."

Gurus of exchange rates have found
An additional coin, small and round,
    Has ended a caper
    With crinkly paper,
While sinking the flotable pound.

    The holiday doll spent a week
    In a swimsuit that played hide and seek.
        She couldn't go wrong
        With a smile and a thong,
    And a bottom that bronzed cheek-to-cheek.

Une fille de Paris was *très bonne*
In a swimsuit she'd hardly got on.
    She displayed such a flair
    On a G-string that there
Were cheers for her cheek - but which one?

    A tourist who fondly believed
    That cocaine down her bra had deceived
        The customs at Dover
        Was firmly done over.
    A drugs bust was what they achieved.

As Venice is wet underfeet,
Engineers have a problem to beat.
No book gives a clue
As to what they should do
If a water main bursts in the street.

BUCK HOUSE BLUES

A Yank who had been to Buck House
Said, "I've not seen the Queen or her spouse.
I don't think it's funny:
It cost me good money.
Disneyworld guarantees Mickey Mouse."

Muffled sobs were observed by a fraction
Of the crowds who'd caused royal reaction.
"It's all gone too far!
My name's E II R!
I'm the Queen, not a tourist attraction!"

There were rumours that chances were fading
That the public could go on invading
Buckingham Palace.
They said (without malice),
That the Queen had been done, Sunday trading.

There was nothing a fellow could do
When the Queen, Duke and dogs came to view
His flat in a mews.
He couldn't refuse:
He'd visited THEM in a queue.

On the steps at Clovelly, take heed,
If you think you can climb them at speed:
There's a place where you ask
For an oxygen mask
And a spot where your nose starts to bleed.

Holiday Time

Fred, on a trip to Uganda,
Fell in love with a lass called Amanda.
She was just like his mum,
And Fred, being dumb,
Was amazed that his dad couldn't standa.

Italians, you will agree,
Are a great deal too complex for me.
They give me a fright
As they drive on the right,
And their hot taps are all labelled C.*

* The Italian for hot is *calde*.

A tripper, returning to Kenya,
Was told, "They don't want to demenya,
But the lions on the plain
Say, don't come again,
On account of they've already senya."

Said a lady, while visiting Rye,
"Does anyone understand why
It's not Wheat or Barley?
I'll have to ask Charley,
And wait for his waspish reply."

There's a girl from the country, called Phoebe,
Who bain't near as bright as what whoebe.
In Rome, the Pope's blessing
Just left the lass guessing.
"And who", murmured Phoebe, "might hoebe?"

Visitors find Saskatchewan
Far more of a bane than a bchewan.
The natives look at you when
You call it Saskatchewan,
Which is why tourists leave pretty schewan.

A guest who had thought it quite bright
To dive in the pool at first light,
        Alas, so it goes,
        Bashed his brain through his toes:
The thing had been drained overnight.

THREE OF A KIND

A cannibal went home and swore,
"Self-catering hols are a bore!
        You see me reduced
        To my head, as I used
To feel hungry and fancy some more."

A much-travelled cannibal said,
"Self-catering holidays led
        To my tending to eat
        An abundance of meat -
Which is why I'm just left with my head."

A cannibal tripper to Spain
Will never go back there again:
        Cost an arm and a leg;
        Got him known as The Peg.
Self-catering hols are a pain.

***

XXXVII

A MESSAGE MISTAKEN

OUR suicide pact was just great.
It was meant to avoid all debate
And to give me the bliss
Of our ultimate kiss -
Not this note saying, "Sorry, can't wait."

Said a punch-packing lady in Leith,
Who had popped out to buy her son's wreath,
"It's the one I assails
For biting his nails:
I just meant to knock out his teeth."

Jack was proud, with his new girl on show.
"What's her name?" Fred said, clearly aglow.
Jack answered, "Chantelle."
Fred said, "Go to hell!
It was just that I wanted to know."

A quick-tempered type in Lahore
Slipped down in some dung on the floor -
Exactly like Matt,
Who exclaimed, "I did that!"
And was instantly thumped on the jaw.

With a code in his doze down in Clwyd,
There lurked by mistake an old Drwyd.
When told he should be
In Llanfair PG,
He answered, "I bloobid well knwyd!"

A Message Mistaken

Rapid flicks of the knife-thrower's wrist
Burst balloons simply hand over fist.
Then an axe thudded near
His assistant's right ear,
And everyone shouted, "He's missed!"

Two packets of loose Cheddar led
To surprise when a customer said,
"Put an *NZ* now, please,
On the New Zealand cheese",
And the manager drew a hen's head.

Flying saucer reports led to folks'
Combing the fields at Four Oaks.
Then the vicar stood up
With a 10ft-high cup
And said that they might be a hoax.

A mischievous monk had some fun,
Introducing a priest to a nun,
Saying, "Father, meet Mother."
They said to each other,
"Good heavens! So this is your son!"

Sarah said, "It would be very good
To agree on monogomy. Could
You give me your view:
Does it matter to you?"
Fred told her, "I'm not into wood."

Said the rector, "The chapel intends
Simultaneous services, friends -
Involving, perhaps,
The altar and apse,
With babies baptised at both ends."

XXXVIII

THE HUMAN CONDITION

DON'T ever dare do that again!
If you're tempted to, kindly refrain!
People pointed and spluttered,
And stood back and muttered,
And then wanted ME to explain!

Dyslexia, quaintly, is not
User-friendly, which means that a lot
Of sufferers find
It isn't inclined
To help them to spell what they've got.

A Martian in Britain would say,
Of the headgear fad that holds sway,
That reversed baseball caps
Are showing, perhaps,
That heads aren't screwed on the right way.

Life's a disease, so it's said,
And it's terminal, whether it's led
In billing and cooing
Or killing and booing:
You know in the end you'll be dead.

For three things, I've no memory - yet
Only one of them gets me upset.
I'm hopeless on faces
As well as on places.
The third, I'm afraid, I forget.

What routines weight-awareness devises!
Thinking thin, looking fat, heaving thighses!
    Exercises each day,
    Then observe rites of weigh
Which say what your size is. More sighses!

    Pseudo-masochists never descend
    To hurting themselves or a friend.
        They blush to explain,
        "It's a bit of a pain -
    But really, we only pretend."

DON'T BE DAFT!

Mens sana in corpore sano
Is achieved when you play with Meccano.
    You make a big trolley,
    Or similar folly,
And run with it round Lake Lugano.

With *corpus* now *sanum*, that's jolly:
If sponsored, you've raised lots of lolly.
    But *sana* your *mens*?
    That largely depends
On if you're adjudged off your trolley.

    Nutritional experts who share
    The facts of their findings declare
        They've frequently found
        That folks who are round
    Are round many meals that are square.

What runs in the family owes
The fact to a factor that flows.
    It generally means
    Generations of genes -
Or a cold, in the case of the nose.

The Human Condition

The troubles of age, as time passes,
Bring strife to each sex and all classes.
Knees buckle, belt won't;
Without glasses, you don't
Have an earthly of finding your glasses.

GUESS WHO

A philosopher, downing a drink,
Said, "Existence has gone on the blink.
I don't give a damn
That I think and so am:
Just am I the I that I think?"

Just think about this, as it's true:
A quite awful option's in view.
It could easily be,
If he isn't he,
He just may turn out to be you.

One assumes that the flab-fighting Brit
Does his diet-jog-exercise bit
So we can all say
At the end of the day,
"Yes, he's dead - but at least he was fit."

Strong though my glasses may be,
At my age, it gets harder to see.
I'm confused when I look
In my little black book:
All the names seem to end in *MD*.

Splinters in thumbs, there's no doubt,
Are what getting old is about.
To be seen, they must be
At arm's length from me,
So I can't reach to get the things out.

The Human Condition

Hypochondriacs, it is well known,
Consider themselves to be prone
        To illness and blight -
        And prove that they're right
By getting their names on a stone.

        No wonder we're stressed, as a race.
        Just look at the problem we face:
                If we don't keep the full
                Gravitational pull,
        We'll simply float off into space.

XXXIX

LIFE AT LARGE

A credit card's worth will depend
On who gets it out for the spend.
In wrong hands, helpful plastic
Behaves something drastic.
Well, it's known as your flexible friend.

COMMERCIAL UNIONS

**A bright lad, perhaps one of Mensa's,
Said two Royal weddings made sense as
Anne became Mark's,
Prompting bands in the parks,
And then prompting Charles to be Spencer's.**

**This royal commercialised factor
Was bound in the end to extract a
Response. Cried Prince Andy:
"A Ferguson's handy!
Attract her! Attract her!** ***A tractor. . ?"***

A hesitant speech is a cause
Of all-round dismay - and it bores!
It's human to *". . .er"*,
But people prefer
To finish to gales of applause.

Life at Large

Perpetual motion, my dears,
Is too much for man, it appears.
Neither has he
The skill of a tree,
To stand without moving for years.

The Rabumps had a daughter whom they
Christened Tiara one day.
She's had to refuse
To live in a mews:
(Tiara Rabump, 2A. . .)

A gnome which was hurled from the shelf
By its owner, declared to itself:
"I have now achieved blast-off.
This man's gnome is his cast-off.
I shall claim on the old National Elf."

The ballot box loses its grip
On the course of democracy's ship:
Put a cross, which is right,
(A tick's wrong) and it's quite
Certain you'll give it the slip.

When yobs act like pigs, it disposes
Observers to say this discloses
Beyond refutation
A clear explanation
Of why they wear rings through their noses.

Nouvelle cuisine makes us feel
Uplifted by visual appeal.
It's costly but pretty:
It just seems a pity
It can't be described as a meal.

Life at Large

Haute couture is unwearable clothes
On parade at incestuous shothes,
    Inspiring what's spent
    On overpriced scent,
For which you will pay through the nothes.

Superstition will always amuse a
Sceptic who says it's a loser.
    What faith can you put
    In an old rabbit's foot
Which failed its original user?

A villain from old Albuquerque,
With a record decidedly merque,
    Earned a criminal living,
    But every Thanksgiving
Went home for his share of the terque.

Americans call their kids "honey",
Acknowledging that they cost money
    And come as a jar
    And spread far too far
While sticky and not at all funny.

A statistical pair drove you wild,
Unless you just nodded and smiled:
    With two kids, nicely spaced,
    Was one stopped at the waist.
They explained, "It's our two-point-fourth child."

Said Fred, who was roughly aged three,
"A thunderstorm's lovely to see!
    I don't find it frightening
    When lightning is brightening:
That's God, taking pictures of me."

. . . in her knickers' elastic

Life at Large

A sex bomb whose figure's fantastic
Has altered her shape something drastic.
    She's not looked the same
    Since her dad's zimmer frame
Got stuck in her knickers' elastic

    A woman addicted to rice
    Is urgently seeking advice.
        She says that she's tried
        Long-grain boiled and fried,
    But asks if rice *paper* is nice.

A kiss-of-life doll they call Clare
Gives first aid exponents a scare.
    In tentative ventures,
    She swallows their dentures
And throws both her legs in the air.

    Said Tex, who'd been sitt'n surmis'n,
    "I guess that I find it surpris'n
        That, fast though I drive,
        I never arrive
    Any place near the horiz'n."

Breaking off from a kiss with delight,
Fred declared, "You're a bit of all right!
    What a smacker! Oh, brother!
    Do you fancy another?"
She said, "Yes, but he's busy tonight."

    Some charmers take men and they twist 'em
    So coyly that none can resist 'em.
        But a lady in Halifax
        Despatched such a palifax,
    Replies simply gummed up the system.

Life at Large

Santa Claus says he's no cause to sing
Of the joys that the season should bring.
Christmas Eve, poor old crock
Always hangs up his sock;
Christmas Morning, he's not got a thing.

Said a man of inordinate wealth,
"I never do good deeds by stealth.
I firmly believe
All the praise I receive
Improves my well-being and health."

Though smoking brings coughs that are hacky
And all sorts of things much more tacky,
Bacchanalian revels
For kids, little devils,
Will still back an alien baccy.

An impossible poser called Dan
Beguiled a young thing from Cwmbran.
The one common factor
That seemed to attract her
Was. . . both of them loved the same man.

When buying a bra, it's a must
That a girl gives tradition her trust.
Mum knows a bra's best
When applied to the chest,
So that's why the rule's *Fit to Bust.*

A somewhat despairing old prune
Told the mouth that it faced from a spoon,
"As a healthy young plum,
I'd no clue that I'd come
To my fate as a wrinkly so soon."

Life at Large

Said a bashful young lady from Street,
“A radish is lovely to eat,
But when I partake,
The noise that I make
Is one I don’t like to repeat.”

Cried a diner one night in Porthcawl,
“I don’t like this soup much at all!
Waiter, here just a minute!
What’s that fly doing in it?”
Said the waiter, “I think it’s the crawl.”

In Hector*, the tax man was blest
With a voice: “Self-assessment is best!”
He said, “Don’t delay
When the time comes to pay.”
Hectoring’s what he did best.

* The cartoon character in a bowler hat, introduced in 1996 to herald the introduction of self-assessment taxation.

Paddy’s broad brogue gave a clue
To long years in Cork, and you knew
The source of that squeaking
While Paddy was speaking:
That wide-fitting old Irish shoe.

A man of inordinate wealth
Said, “I never do good deeds by stealth.
I’d be bursting to cry,
‘I’m a wonderful guy!’
And frustration’s not good for my health.”

Life at Large

A fire-fighter foolishly gazes
In the eyes of a lass he dismays. "Is
    There any hope, Brenda,
    That you'll love me tender?"
The lass, alas, says, "Go to blazes."

There's a middle-aged lady from Sutton
Whose fashion sense misses the button;
    Says she gives not a damn:
    Mutton dressed up as lamb
Beats mutton that's dressed up as mutton.

The ubiquitous p is a fetter
The euro could change for the better.
    (Since we haven't the sense
    To say *penny* or *pence*,
Our currency unit's a letter).

There's a fellow whose cocktail quips
Fail to charm any chick as she sips.
    Between sips, her lips say,
    "You're a bore - go away!"
Between sighs, her eyes say, "Read my lips."

Insisting, "*I'll come to no harm!*",
He stepped from a plane over Guam.
    He ought to have known
    That he'd drop like a stone:
He should have tried flapping an arm.

For a few days in spring, the magnolia
Has glorious blooms to consolia
    For the winter you've had.
    Rejoice and be glad:
'til next winter comes, it's just folia.

XL

THE LIMEREMIL

The Limeremil will soon, I'll be bound,
Make doggerelists' muse run aground.
Every line that you hunt
Has to rhyme back-to-front,
As well as the proper way round.

UNDERSTAND what we're trying to do:
Land a feat that we're thinking is new.
To write in reverse,
You have to rehearse,
And check rhymes and scansion twice, too.

do to trying/ we're what/ Understand:
new is/ thinking that/ feat a Land.
reverse/ in write To
rehearse/ to have You
too twice/ scansion and/ rhymes check And.

Go to! Competition's intense!
No prospect here for the dense!
Make palindrome ploy:
Take time to enjoy,
So what is seen backwards makes sense.

intense/ Competition's to Go!
dense/ the for here/ prospect No!
ploy pal/ indrome Make:
enjoy/ to time Take,
sense makes/ backwards seen/ is what So.

The Limeremil

That surely's a task that will need
Flat-footed hard work and no speed.
    Why not in this rhyme?
    I haven't the time:
Cat out of bag, we've sown seed!

need will/ that task a/ surely's That
speed no/ and work hard/ footed-Flat
    rhyme this/ in not Why?
    time the/ haven't I;
Seed sown/ we've bag the/ of out Cat!

IMPOSSIBILIMEREMIL?

The stage is now set! Things are tense!
The limerick's next move can commence!
    It's time to rehearse
    Creating a verse
Which, reversed, rhymes and scans AND MAKES SENSE!

***

FAILED-AGAIN FOOTNOTE

Rotten Haystacks: the explanation

Slime is a word I'd forgotten.
Alas, all this verse I've begotten -
These sweat-bedewed limericks -
Can't be called Slimericks:
They'd just look like haystacks gone rotten.

John Slim

INDEX OF FIRST LINES

A dapper new surgeon appeared	The National Health
A dazed etymologist said	The World of Words
A deaf boffin's failure to follow	The National Health
A dental mechanic in Dover	The National Health
A dentist, while living in Louth	The National Health
A diffident cowboy called Frame	Merely Males
A disconsolate lass, Freya Clare	The World of Words
A divinity student said he	Religious Disorders
A dog's a divine indication	Animal Antics
A don who was one of Emmanuel's	The Demon Drink
A drink where you're needing some *nous* is	The Demon Drink
A drunk, nearly out on his feet	The Demon Drink
A duchess who takes tea at Claridge's	The World of Words
A dyslexic agnostic called Hogg	Reversals
A factor that merits applause is	Merely Males
A fanciful woman called Eva	Shall We Join the Ladies?
A farm student, down in Torbay	Life on the Land
A far-sighted Boeing mechanic	Logical Lapses
A fearless explorer once said	Holiday Time
A fed-up psychologist found	The National Health
A fellow who cuddled a croc	Animal Antics
A fellow with failed self-delusion	Merely Males
A fellow with minimal brain	Merely Males
A female whose figure gets bigure	Shall We Join the Ladies?
A fire and a saddle complete	The World of Words
A fire-fighter foolishly gazes	Life at Large
A fishpond is there to enjoy	Animal Antics
A football philosopher, Job	Biblical Bits
A forgetful old fellow from Fakenham	Merely Males
A frantic young fellow from Skye	Merely Males
A friendly young dancer called Kate	Occupational Hazards
A fruit-picker, down on all fours	Signs of Uncertainty
A gardening expert called Tranter	Life on the Land
A gardening novice in Ware	Life on the Land
A ghost in the Eagle and Star	A Chance of a Ghost
A ghost who was new said, "I'm bored!	A Chance of a Ghost
A ghost who was whiter than white	A Chance of a Ghost
A gnome which was hurled from the shelf	Life at Large

A golfer with fine self-delusion	Sporting Gestures
A group of invisible menders	Occupational Hazards
A guest who had thought it quite bright	Holiday Time
A happy inventor in Troon	Domestic Issues
A hard-working jogger from Skye	Merely Males
Ahead of's becoming a bore	The Media
A health food fanatic called Gus	Merely Males
A helpful young fellow from Skye	The World of Words
A he-man complained, "There will be	Imperfectly Correct
A hesitant speech is a cause	Life at Large
A hidebound old chap from Braemar	The World of Words
A high-speed young fellow from Brum	The World of Words
A holidaymaker called Vera	Holiday Time
A holidaymaker from Clee	Holiday Time
A horse-loving laddie called Keith	Logical Lapses
A hospital porter in Crewe	The National Health
A humourless poet, a bore	Literary Leanings
A hundred-and-one, six and *fifty*	The World of Words
A kindly young curate called Walter	Religious Disorders
A kiss-of-life doll they call Clare	Life at Large
A lady in 'Frisco near died	One for the Road
A lady quite truly devout	The Demon Drink
A lavatory cleaner named Nell	Occupational Hazards
Aldwych tube station's procession	The World of Words
A legendary lass called Miss Muffet	Cursory Nursery
A limbless explorer once said	A Little Learning
A limerick writer in Looe	Literary Leanings
A Lincolnshire lad saw the frost on	The World of Words
A literate hack is quite rare	The Media
A lively young lady called Zoe	The World of Words
All glory and honour is yours	Religious Disorders
All high-wire walkers ignore	Occupational Hazards
All the same, what he did was sincere	King Lear
Alopecia, of course, is not rare	Merely Males
A lovely young lady called Sue	Signs of Uncertainty
Alphabetically speaking, you may	The World of Words
Alternative funny men say	Imperfectly Correct
Although I am possibly dumb, what	Domestic Issues
Although Riverdance is upbeat	All for Art

Although she quite failed to disarm a	Anarchic Anagrams
Although you can say, *Still the sinking*	A Slip of the Tongue
A magnificent batting display	Sporting Gestures
A man called today on a camel	Animal Antics
A man for whom everything shows	Merely Males
A man looked a bit of a freak	Religious Disorders
A man of inordinate wealth	Life at Large
A man with a face like a ferret	Merely Males
A man with a very long face	A Lengthy Business
A man with a very long foot	A Lengthy Business
A man with a very long name	A Lengthy Business
A man with a very long neck	A Lengthy Business
A man with a very long nose	A Lengthy Business
A man with a very long pause	A Lengthy Business
A man with a very long way	A Lengthy Business
A man with four legs and a beak	Merely Males
A marriage may lack the ability	Marriage Lines
A Martian in Britain would say	The Human Condition
Ambulatory craze	The World of Words
American experts could see	The World of Words
Americans call their kids "honey"	Life at Large
A mischievous monk had some fun	A Message Mistaken
A mobile phone will deny	Domestic Issues
Among all life's urgent demands	The World of Words
Among that which follows, you can	Introduction
A motor you cannot rely on	One for the Road
A much-travelled cannibal said	Holiday Time
A musical man from the Hallé	The World of Words
Amusing though limericks may be	A Health Warning
An actor, achieving an aim	The World of Words
Anagrams, caught in the raw	Anarchic Anagrams
An amateur gardening nut	Logical Lapses
An amateur sailor called Porter	Sporting Gestures
An ambitious young barrister, Toya	Lawful Occasions
A native of Southern Jahore	One for the Road
An aubrieta complained, "I'm a flower	The World of Words
A newsreader said, "I deplore	The Media
An expert in polished titanium	Merely Males
An explorer, safe home in Nuneaton	A Little Learning

As he painted his ultimate poppy	All for Art
As it's known that the mind has a flaw	Merely Males
Ask any artist around	The World of Words
A small boy in France may aver	The World of Words
A smooth-tongued attorney whose grip	Lawful Occasions
A sociable Scot in Siam	Merely Males
A somewhat despairing old prune	Life at Large
A statistical pair drove you wild	Life at Large
As the stars of the show took a bough	All for Art
A strawberry-picker said, "Please!"	Signs of Uncertainty
A student of English at Hook	A Little Learning
A studious young fellow called Ray	A Little Learning
A sunny young man at Loch Ness	Merely Males
A surgeon of limited vision	The National Health
As Venice is wet underfeet	Holiday Time
A sweet-smelling Zurich-based gnome	Domestic Issues
As we know flight recorders stand shocks	Logical Lapses
A tenor sax scrum-half sought fun	Sporting Gestures
A thoroughly unimpressed sheep	Animal Antics
A thousand-and-nine, with no tricks	The World of Words
A tourist in Wales murmured, "Cor!	Signs of Uncertainty
A tourist who fondly believed	Holiday Time
A tradition that surgeons won't break	The National Health
A tripper, returning to Kenya	Holiday Time
At the weepiest wedding for years	Marriage Lines
Aubrieta's a name that we say	The World of Words
A VCR's role is to break	Domestic Issues
A verse-writing fellow from Glos	The World of Words
A very bald gentleman said	Merely Males
A very old fellow in Ryde	Merely Males
A villain from old Albuquerque	Life at Large
A wealthy old buffer in Mayfair	Merely Males
A willing young man in Redhill	The Demon Drink
A wine connoisseur, name of Plunkett	Logical Lapses
A wise leader-writer's inclined	The Media
A wise old owl who was asked why	Logical Lapses
A wise poultry farmer said, "When	Life on the Land
A woman addicted to rice	Life at Large
A word game, a sort of a sport	The World of Words

Getting down on all fours is one more — The World of Words
Getting words back-to-front is a chore — Reversals
"Gigantic Boot Sale" means we'll meet — Signs of Uncertainty
God forbid we should sound too progressive — One for the Road
Going head-over-heels, it's been found — The World of Words
Goldilocks' fame found its origin — Cursory Nursery
Golfers and anglers all vie — Sporting Gestures
Good neighbours bring joy that's immense — Domestic Issues
Go to! Competition's intense! — The Limeremil
"Graham Taylor for England!" they cried — Anarchic Anagrams
Gurus of exchange rates have found — Holiday Time
Gushed a lush in a seaside resort — The Demon Drink
Guy is a word which once meant — The World of Words

H*ANDYPERSON required.* What a joke! — Imperfectly Correct
Has anyone here understood — The World of Words
H-A/-S-R-H/-Y-M-E — A Concentrated Spell
Haute couture is unwearable clothes — Life at Large
Have you heard what's occurred with the surd — A Little Learning
Hell's taking a long time to burn! Oh — Religious Disorders
Henry the pooch could not quell — Animal Antics
Her is a word that is said — The World of Words
Her swain doesn't often drink hooch — Domestic Issues
Hill farmers, it's easy to tell — Life on the Land
His stethoscope clamped to his head — The National Health
His travels in various areas — Merely Males
How can every Jumbo defy — Logical Lapses
Howdah is short for a bit — Animal Antics
Hypochondriacs, it is well known — The Human Condition

IF Bangor were given a nought — The World of Words
I fear that it could be a bore — King Lear
If the first year AD was year none — Logical Lapses
If you drink when you're driving, you've built — One for the Road
If you grieve that they're clean, please take heart — Introduction
If you look for a rhyme based on Tucson — The World of Words
I have yet to discover the relevance — Animal Antics
"I'll explain my proposal like this — The World of Words
"I'm dismayed!" Fred exclaimed to his mother — Merely Males

In Boston, the burghers saw stars — One for the Road
In church, the bride's mother said, "Dear — Marriage Lines
In Hector, the tax man was blest — Life at Large
In one of their small-hours debates — Animal Antics
In Parma, an actor named Sam — All for Art
In Sheffield, the Reverend Brain gave — Religious Disorders
Insisting, "I'll come to no harm!" — Life at Large
In snooker, when aiming, they call — Sporting Gestures
In spite of his governess-aunt — Just Back in Time
Intelligent sailors like me — Logical Lapses
Intense/ Competition's to Go! — The Limeremil
In the bar, a white horse soon saw red — Animal Antics
In the bath, Archimedes knew why the — Just Back in Time
In the bridal suite, evening approached — Marriage Lines
In the dungeons, a peasant from Bradley — Just Back in Time
In *The Merchant of Venice*, we saw — Literary Leanings
Invaded, he's apt to inveigh — The World of Words
In verses, together they make — Introduction
Istanbul's crooked cobbler is prosperous — Occupational Hazards
Italian food, one can show — The World of Words
Italians, you will agree — Holiday Time
I think you may finally flip — A Slip of the Tongue
It is kind of the cactus-type dahlia — Domestic Issues
It isn't too hard to discern a — The World of Words
It's a curse! Let's rehearse, to explore — Reversals
It's as well that two men of resource — Sporting Gestures
It's clear, though it seems rather trite — The World of Words
It's clever, how traders design — Occupational Hazards
It's easy to see in a trice — Imperfectly Correct
It's good that two lords could agree — The World of Words
It's known as a mobile phone — Domestic Issues
It was terribly easy to sneer — Merely Males
I've Arrived and can show you the proof — The Media
I've heard fish described as a dish — Logical Lapses
"I've nothing to do", said Fred's brother — The World of Words

JACK was proud, with his new girl on show — A Message Mistaken
J Caesar would never agree — Just Back in Time

Jeune fille qui habite a Rouen The World of Words
Joan of Arc, wife of Noah, said, "Let's bring" Biblical Bits
John Constable said, "There might be All for Art
Jonah sets out for a sail Biblical Bits
J-U/-S-T-A/-S-P-E A Concentrated Spell
Just think about this, as it's true The Human Condition
Just why doesn't *wash* rhyme with *ash?* The World of Words

KAMIKAZE'S for those who like flying Occupational Hazards
King Alfred tried hard to create Just Back in Time
King Harold, a barrel of woes Just Back in Time
King Harold's last words, so they say Just Back in Time
King's Men, who are unfeeling folk Cursory Nursery

LABOUR or Liberal or Tory The World of Words
Laisser faire is a term I have known The World of Words
Las Vegas is where the lass gave Anarchic Anagrams
Letters unite, side by side Anarchic Anagrams
Lexicographers, as they reflect The World of Words
Lexicographers clearly aren't bright The World of Words
Lexicographers no longer try The World of Words
Licensed's the word that's the biz Signs of Uncertainty
Life's a disease, so it's said The Human Condition
Life was designed as an idyll Musical Items
Likewise, the content's an art Literary Leanings
Limericks deter infiltration The World of Words
Limericks have never quite been Introduction
Limericks lurk undetected The World of Words
Linguistics mean little to Bill The World of Words
Lisped Sally, "I know I'm a dunth The World of Words
Little Miss Muffet sat on a Cursory Nursery
Little Miss Muffet, they say Cursory Nursery
Llanfair/pwllgwy/syllgo- The World of Words
Lot's sceptical outlook grew rife Biblical Bits
Luddites of language will say The World of Words

MPs cry "'ear,'ear!" amid cheers The World of Words
MPs never know where they're landing Occupational Hazards
MPs who "make perfectly clear" The World of Words

First line	Section
Macbeth is a thane full of pain	Literary Leanings
Male torsos grow older and vary	Merely Males
Man is a word being banned	Imperfectly Correct
Meet is a four-letter word	The World of Words
Memo re speeder A Short	Correspondence Course
Mens sana in corpore sano	The Human Condition
Michelangelo - he was a sweetie	All for Art
Mixed infants, when drawing their God	A Little Learning
Modern art caused a hell of a stir	All for Art
Moreover, there's no-one who'll haggle	Literary Leanings
Moreover, without cock and bull	Introduction
Motorway morons defy the	One for the Road
Muffled sobs were observed by a fraction	Holiday Time
Mum looked at the turkey. "Oh, heck!	Domestic Issues
My pig and I go for a walk	My Pig
My pig does not usually cry	My Pig
My pig gets himself in a state	My Pig
My pig has shown helpful complicity	My Pig
My pig is a beast I admire	My Pig
My pig is a glorious beast	My Pig
My pig is a gullible guy	My Pig
My pig is a pig of resource	My Pig
My pig is a pig you can hail	My Pig
My pig is as fit as a fiddle	My Pig
My pig just recoiled in confusion	My Pig
My pig loves his food - he's a nut. He	My Pig
My pig said, "I hope you don't mind	My Pig
My pig said, "I'm feeling quite bitter	My Pig
My pig said, "These feet I have got	My Pig
My pig thought he'd sail on the sea	My Pig
My pig told his grandmother, "Nan	My Pig
My pig was as chuffed as could be	My Pig
My pig, who quite likes to decide	My Pig
NANCY KERRIGAN suffered a jar	Anarchic Anagrams
Need will/ that task a/ surely's That	The Limeremil
Newton's Law soon ensured its longevity	Logical Lapses
New Year's Eve, '99, the world thought	Logical Lapses
Nobody doubted the mission	Just Back in Time

No explanation is known	The World of Words
Nouvelle cuisine makes us feel	Life at Large
No wonder we're stressed, as a race	The Human Condition
N-T makes a sound past the ken	Literary Leanings
Nutritional experts who share	The Human Condition
OH, Fanny, a happy release	The Media
Oh, Terry, Patricia, you're ratty! Oh	The World of Words
Old Harold believes Joan of Arc	Old Harold
Old Harold believes opera's need	Old Harold
Old Harold had finished his chore	Old Harold
Old Harold's a bit of a mutt	Old Harold
Old Harold's a devil for whist	Old Harold
Old Harold says bathrooms can't beat	Old Harold
Old Harold says joy is complete	Old Harold
Old Harold surprised an old flame	Old Harold
Old Harold was out with the boys	Old Harold
Old Mother Hubbard, who went to	Cursory Nursery
On a winding road, chances are few	One for the Road
One assumes that the flab-fighting Brit	The Human Condition
One day, at a wedding in Canaan	Biblical Bits
One thing we discover, alas, is	All for Art
On his wedding day, Fred made it clear	Marriage Lines
On the Isle of Capri, where Frank drank	The World of Words
On the road to Damascus, young Saul	Biblical Bits
On the steps at Clovelly, take heed	Holiday time
Our cricketers don't have to try	Sporting Gestures
Our suicide pact was just great	A Message Mistaken
Our tortoise was shy, we could tell	Animal Antics
P*ADDLE your own canoe*	The World of Words
Paddy's broad brogue gave a clue	Life at Large
Paradoxical language compounds	The World of Words
Parking is always a fiddle	One for the Road
Paul Gascoigne's post-Wembley reward	Anarchic Anagrams
Paul Gascoigne, turned about face	Anarchic Anagrams
Pedestrian precincts don't fuss	One for the Road
People agree without question	One for the Road
People who've never learned how	The World of Words

Perpetual motion, my dears — Life at Large
"Plant ties", said the placard. Fred glowered — Signs of Uncertainty
"Please, doctor", said Fred, "I'm perplexed — Merely Males
Please, why aren't my biscuit tins square? — Domestic Issues
Poems today, heaven knows — Literary Leanings
Poems today rarely rhyme — Literary Leanings
Prayer is a thing that's been hit — Religious Disorders
Pre-conditions are now in position — The World of Words
Presumably, part of the charm — Signs of Uncertainty
Professional boxers? Insane! — Sporting Gestures
Propinquity CAN be a strain — Domestic Issues
Proud Pisans quite rightly insisted — Holiday time
Pseudo-masochists never descend — The Human Condition
"Put your shirt on that horse", they all said — Sporting Gestures

QUASIMODO was not pleased at all — Literary Leanings

RABBIE BURNS, it is clear, didn't care — Literary Leanings
Rabbie Burns, that implacable poet — Literary Leanings
Rapid flicks of the knife-thrower's wrist — A Message Mistaken
Regardless of age, race or sex — Occupational Hazards
"Religion's decidedly odd — Religious Disorders
Rosaline was a young woman who — The World of Words
Rotavator's a word that can cater — Reversals
Rotten Haystacks: the title may send — Rotten Haystacks
Round about now should allow — The World of Words
Rugby's ball is an oval one, which — Sporting Gestures

SAID a bashful young lady from Street — Life at Large
Said a bellringer, ringing in Cheam — Occupational Hazards
Said a case-hardened mother from Crewe — Domestic Issues
Said a cow to a sheep in the dark — Animal Antics
Said a curious elephant, "Spell — Animal Antics
Said Adam, "I don't want to crib — Biblical Bits
Said Adam one morning to Eve — Biblical Bits
Said a distant relation of mine — Shall We Join the Ladies?
Said a fellow from Leamington Spa — Logical Lapses
Said a fellow named Fawkes, "This is why — Just Back in Time

Said a forceful young woman from Bicester	Imperfectly Correct
Said a glow-worm, "I don't feel right	Animal Antics
Said a happy young butterfly, "Few	Animal Antics
Said a journalist down in Torquay	The Media
Said a lad whom good grace had deserted	The Demon Drink
Said a lady, while visiting Rye	Holiday Times
Said a lady whose snoring had led	Domestic Issues
Said a lover of language called Rory	The World of Words
Said a man of inordinate wealth	Life at Large
Said a man with a band on his head	Merely Males
Said a miserable fellow from Cork	Merely Males
Said an actor in Burnham-on-Sea	All for Art
Said an anxious young man from St Just	Merely Males
Said an idle young man from Tralee	Literary Leanings
Said a novice, "Life's fun, in the main	Religious Disorders
Said an upright young lady named Win	The Demon Drink
Said a peg-legged groundsman, "I force	Sporting Gestures
Said a poet who came from Madras	The World of Words
Said a Pole to a Finn, "Don't demolish	The World of Words
Said a punch-packing lady in Leith	A Message Mistaken
Said a racehorse, "It's got out of hand	Sporting Gestures
Said a Sassenach, trapped in Dunoon	Musical Items
Said a student of language in Bray	Imperfectly Correct
Said a vicar, invited to look	A Chance of a Ghost
Said a watt to an ohm, "I don't know	A Little Learning
Said a weak-willed old fellow called Dewar	Merely Males
Said a word-blind young man from Lee Bank	Merely Males
Said Beethoven, "People prefer	Musical Items
Said Daisy the cow, with a gloat	Animal Antics
Said Dorothy, there in Glengarry	Domestic Issues
Said Eve, "All right, things do look grim	Biblical Bits
Said Fred, "I would like some advice	Animal Antics
Said Fred, who was roughly aged three	Life at Large
Said Henry VIII, "I declare"	Just Back in Time
Said His Honour, "The trouble with me	Lawful Occasions
Said Katie, "How do you enhance a	Domestic Issues
Said Maisie, "The beauty of sin	The Demon Drink
Said Michael, who came from Tralee	The Demon Drink
Said Naomi, "Though I have grown	Reversals

Said Susie, "I smoke, you can tell	Domestic Issues
Said Tex, who'd been sitt'n surmis'n	Life at Large
Said the doctor, "I'm sure that the cause	Animal Antics
Said the herdsman, "I've been born and bred	Life on the Land
Said the Lord, "Let us not buck the trends	Religious Disorders
Said the midwife, "Your labour, by rights	The National Health
Said the rector, "The chapel intends	A Message Mistaken
Said Vincent Van Gogh, "It's a blow	All for Art
Sale signs could well prove to be sprats	Signs of Uncertainty
Sammy Snail gave his mother a hug	Animal Antics
Santa Claus says he's no cause to sing	Life at Large
Sarah said, "It would be very good	A Message Mistaken
Saying Llanfair in full is a deli-	The World of Words
Saying Llanfair/pwllgwy/syllgo-	The World of Words
Saying musical names isn't wise. It	Musical Items
Security lamps are a lark	Domestic Issues
Selective weedkillers affect	Domestic Issues
September, remember, returns	The World of Words
Sewing's a craft that's so pure	The World of Words
Sheepdogs in trials induce sleep	Life on the Land
She explained that by being a Ms	Imperfectly Correct
Sherlock Holmes always worked out the plots on	Literary Leanings
She started to say, for a joke	A Slip of the Tongue
Short words with the ending *A-R*	The World of Words
Simon will climb and then stop	Sporting Gestures
Since home is the place you reside	The World of Words
Since phones first went mobile, they've shown	One for the Road
Since *twos* (rhymed with *choose*) proves to be	A Little Learning
Singing praises, O Lord, in full flow	Religious Disorders
Slap-happy Stanley adores	Anarchic Anagrams
Slime is a word I'd forgotten	Failed-Again Footnote
Soccer pundits have surely rehearsed	The Media
So Fanny has gone for her harp	The Media
Some battery hens in Kings Lynn	Life on the Land
Some charmers take men and they twist 'em	Life at Large
Some deep-seated psyche explains	One for the Road
Some funding would help to endorse a	Literary Leanings
Some painters achieve world renown	All for Art
Some women, though oddly at ease	Logical Lapses

Sopranos and tenors are prone	Musical Items
Splinters in thumbs, there's no doubt	The Human Condition
Steve - Bill's son by Diane (his first wife)	Marriage Lines
Strong though my glasses may be	The Human Condition
Sunset View: when we saw it, we knew it	Domestic Issues
Superstition will always amuse a	Life at Large
Supposing you die of starvation	The World of Words
Swimming's a pleasure: you get	Sporting Gestures
TS ELIOT soon started to give a damn	Anarchic Anagrams
Tautology's always the same	The World of Words
That lovely old city of Rheims	A Little Learning
That surely's a task that will need	The Limeremil
That tautologous form of attack	The World of Words
That very strange person, The Chair	Imperfectly Correct
The ageing of man is what shows	Merely Males
The antics of cranks cannot charm a	Imperfectly Correct
The artist asked, "Will you allow	All for Art
The ballot box loses its grip	Life at Large
The bellringer made no apologies	The World of Words
The bell tolls for Greenland - oh, hell!	The World of Words
The bishop, the wicked old blighter	Religious Disorders
The bride's mother anxiously told her	Marriage Lines
The British abroad have no doubt	Holiday Time
The camel said, "Allah is wise	Animal Antics
The Catholic Church does have a slight	Religious Disorders
The challenge is open to you	The World of Words
The Church's particular patter	Religious Disorders
The commentary team haven't stopped	The Media
The crew of an old submarine	Animal Antics
The delivery suite was struck dumb	The National Health
The dish and the spoon had a row	Cursory Nursery
The draper's assistant looked hurt	Occupational Hazards
The English knew what they were doing	The World of Words
The fellows who sing in a choir	Musical Items
The French, as a race, cannot see	Holiday Time
The frigate's MO has a few	The National Health
The front of a queue at a light	One for the Road
The *fugit* that happens to *tempus* is	A Little Learning

The gas board's researchers were bright	Logical Lapses
The ghost of Bill Sikes was agog	A Chance of a Ghost
The greeting was heated, not warm	Merely Males
The guru, 92, said, "How sweet!	Occupational Hazards
The haunting of rural retreats	A Chance of a Ghost
The holiday doll spent a week	Holiday Time
Their coffee was always the source	Domestic Issues
Their friends are all deeply upset	Domestic Issues
Their lunacies now stretch so far	Imperfectly Correct
Their marriage is needing repair	Domestic Issues
The Kerrigan name's on a slice	Anarchic Anagrams
The landlord who rules at the Star	The Demon Drink
The large rusting tank was in situ	Domestic Issues
The Limeremil will soon, I'll be bound	The Limeremil
The limerick does not rely	Literary Leanings
The limerick's space, shape and duration	The World of Words
The locals unite to complain	The Demon Drink
The lollipop lady once said	Occupational Hazards
The loonies' *man* madness will worsen	Imperfectly Correct
The Merchant of Venice's nausea	Literary Leanings
T-H/-E-M-E/-S-S-A	A Concentrated Spell
The Monarch declared, "I have gone	Occupational Hazards
The motor car serves as a cloak	One for the Road
Themself is an ace in the hand	Imperfectly Correct
The night that Fred really got canned	The Demon Drink
The paddock at Ascot has gloss	Sporting Gestures
The pessimist Job said to Moses	Biblical Bits
The phone rang on stage as the cue	All for Art
The Players have done it again	All for Art
The "politically-right" strangely swear	Imperfectly Correct
The Pope said, "I could be a slob	Religious Disorders
The primate, the faithful could see	Religious Disorders
The prostate's the family bane	Shall We Join the Ladies?
The Rabumps had a daughter whom they	Life at Large
There are few who do not understand	Lawful Occasions
There are loonies at large who could harm a	The World of Words
There are those who think tights are sublime	Lawful Occasions
There are those who think walking through walls	A Chance of a Ghost
There isn't an *A*, but an *O*	The World of Words

When baldness begins, what is more	Merely Males
When builders are building a wall	Occupational Hazards
When buying a bra, it's a must	Life at Large
When called to the Bar, Fred said, "Honey	Lawful Occasions
When DID T S Eliot find	Anarchic Anagrams
When do people first make the absurd	Imperfectly Correct
When Higgins (Professor) harangued	The World of Words
When pop groups play live, go in dread	Musical Items
When pushed by a cuckoo he knew	Animal Antics
When putting the choir through its paces	Musical Items
When there's a strange tale to relate	Literary Leanings
When unions unite for a tussle	Occupational Hazards
When yobs act like pigs, it disposes	Life at Large
Where learning makes barely a ripple	A Little Learning
While taking his FRCS	The National Health
While up to his knees in the mire	Life on the Land
While weeding, perspiring, Anstruther	Life on the Land
"Why is this called a boom, Uncle Fred?"	Logical Lapses
William, a tar on a whaler	The World of Words
William Tell made the onlookers gape	Just Back in Time
William Tell's son said, "I smell like this	Just Back in Time
William Tell used to get in a stew	Just Back in Time
With a code in his doze down in Clwyd	A Message Mistaken
With a diet, the whole situation	Logical Lapses
With a humour which possibly leans	Domestic Issues
"With butter and marge", murmured Fred	Domestic Issues
With coffee, they're fearless and frank	Imperfectly Correct
With *corpus* now *sanum*, that's jolly	The Human Condition
With dogs in the dark, when you've got 'em	Animal Antics
With foresight and planning, we ought	Animal Antics
With hurdle race broadcasts, prepare	The Media
With lanes marked for traffic, the growth	One for the Road
With most fish, I've no wish to feel pally but	A Slip of The Tongue
With six Swiss wrist watches, the trick	A Slip of the Tongue
With space being probed, it is worth	A Little Learning
With women, we always expect 'em	Shall We Join the Ladies?
Woody Allen's the name that you need	Anarchic Anagrams
"Words", she averred, "are a bore	The World of Words
Writes Consumer (Confused) of Shoreditch	Domestic Issues
Writing *hung*, meaning *hanged*, even though	The World of Words

YOU had to admire the groom's graces — Marriage Lines
Your life expectation was short — Lawful Occasions
Your most vital needs when embarking — One for the Road
"You uncouth, gormless nincompoop!" storms — Merely Males
You've no earthly reason to grin! — Domestic Issues

ZIMMER *frei* are the words on display — Signs of Uncertainty